WRITING HISTORY

WRITING HISTORY

Local Stories by New Writers

Edited by
Robert Grant Price
and
Shalini Nanayakkara

LIFE RATTLE PRESS TORONTO, CANADA

Writing History
Local Stories by New Writers

Published in Canada by Life Rattle Press, Toronto

First Edition

Copyright 2018 by the contributing authors

Library and Archives Canada Cataloguing in Publication

Writing History: local stories by new writers
/ collected and edited by Robert Grant Price and Shalini Nanayakkara.
(New writers series)

ISBN 978-1-987936-49-0 (pbk.)

1. History--Miscellanea.
2. History--Literary collections
3. History--Canadian--Ontario--Toronto.

I. Price, Robert Grant, 1976-, editor of compilation
II. Nanayakkara, Shalini, 1996-, editor of compilation
III. Series: Life Rattle new writers series

Cover Design by Laurie Kallis
Typeset by Laurie Kallis

CONTENTS

INTRODUCTION

E ach morning, I peer out my apartment window at St. Paul's
Basilica, the centre of the Irish immigrant community that
arrived in Toronto's Corktown neighbourhood in the mid-1800s.

Last year, when I taught a course in writing about history, I used
the basilica as a test case. If I were to write a history about the basilica, how would I go about it?

Over the course of several weeks, I presented students with steps
I'd take to document the history of St. Paul's. I never intended to
actually write a history of the parish, but I was tempted, especially
after learning about the cemetery buried under the pavement behind
the basilica.

The all-but-forgotten cemetery has stymied development. You
see, you can't dig up a cemetery without informing the descend-
ants of the people buried there. But nobody knows who's packed in
the graves under the pavement. All we know is they were poor and
mostly Irish.

One of these days, after I catch up with other writing projects,
I'll write a history of the basilica. But I still have some doubts about

the project. Of all the stories to write and ways to spend my time, why, I wonder, should I write history?

I can list dozens of reasons to read history. At the top of my list is pleasure. Reading history is a pleasure. I want to know who came before me. I want to see their stories play out—even if I already know how the story ends.

But why should I, or anybody, write history?

The easy answer is the same as why to read history: for the pleasure of discovery. To see the world differently. To put our short lives in perspective.

But we also write history to learn how to read history, to understand how historians work and to attempt their work. What teaches understanding and appreciation better than trying to do the thing for yourself? That's where learning happens.

Anybody embarking on a history project—whether for the general public or for the family—should know the dangers of history.

First, there's the ever-present danger of getting the story wrong. History's smudged with the fingerprints of time and human error and rife with mistakes, myths and half-truths. Christopher Columbus is the obvious example. Contrary to the old story, Columbus didn't discover America. Indigenous North Americans were already here, and Vikings made it across the Atlantic before Columbus ever made his trek. And besides, Columbus landed in the Caribbean, not North America. He was nowhere near what we today call "America."

This sort of error can be corrected and that's one job for the historian, to correct the facts. Or to put it another way: to clear off the smudges without adding smudges of their own.

There's another, larger danger that budding historians should know about: the impulse to distort history for partisan purposes.

It's easy to succumb to the desire to tilt history in the favour of our own interests. We see this tilting almost daily, as various interests wrestle for control of 'the narrative' so they can direct 'the discourse.' The fact is that the discipline of history is as good as the memory hole when we use it to score points in today's political arena.

Finally, history writers face the risk of passing over a good story. Historians must determine what deserves the attention of posterity. It's a huge responsibility. So, like other writers, historians must ask themselves, What's a good story to tell?

Fortunately, we're surrounded by good stories. Local histories preserve the past and show how interesting life was for the people who came before us. New writers of history must open their eyes to what's around them and fight the impulse to say interesting history only happens in royal courts and on battlefields. There are plenty of bodies in the backyard waiting for intrepid writers to find and dig up.

The past may be a foreign land, but by reading and writing history we may discover that its inhabitants are not so different from us. If we ask the right questions of our forbearers, they can give us answers that may help us avoid the mistakes they made. By studying history, we might find the past is closer than we think.

That's what happened to me. As I researched the basilica across the way, I discovered that a distant relation of mine—a priest named John Joseph Egan—worked as a rector in the basilica.

I never expected to find that connection. When I did, I saw the basilica was not as distant as I thought it was.

~~~

The four histories presented in this book originated in History and Writing, a class offered through the Professional Writing and

Introduction

Communication Program at the University of Toronto Mississauga. The course demands that students explore the past by researching and writing a focused history. The writers in this book chose to write histories about the communities where they live. In writing local histories, these writers deepened their understanding of home and give a new story to their readers and to the communities featured in these stories.

Robert Grant Price

2018

SIMMERING

The Life, Death and Afterlife of the Preston Springs Hotel

Isaac Maw

When people ask me where I come from, I usually have to mention Waterloo and Kitchener, the two better-known cities that form a tri-city with my hometown of Cambridge, Ontario.

Cambridge itself is a tri-city, too. In 1973, the provincial government amalgamated the towns of Galt, Hespeler and Preston into a composite city, Cambridge. Today, Galt, Hespeler and Preston exist as three distinct boroughs. Each borough has its own people, its own atmosphere. The people of Galt, Hespeler and Preston are proud of their boroughs and sometimes derisive of the others.

I was born at Cambridge Memorial, in Preston, in 1994. My parents took me home to Hespeler. When I was five, we moved outside of Cambridge, and I went to school in a dense Portuguese neighborhood in South Galt. You could say I'm "from" Galt, but to me, Preston is my home. My truest friends lived there. Those Preston curbs were the curbs I sat on, those Preston streets were the streets I skateboarded, and those Preston pizza joints were the spots where I spent my lunch money. So I defend Preston.

Preston is a sleepy old town with a large population of German immigrants. Riverside Park hosts the Canada Day fireworks and the fair. On King Street, visitors will find a historic downtown with well-preserved heritage buildings. Like every other town in Ontario, it has a war memorial. But Preston has one downfall: odours. In the south end, you can catch a whiff of the waste treatment facility. The north reeks of sulfur. This is the one flaw of my otherwise beautiful hometown: she has bad breath.

But if you truly "rep" Preston, from Preston Heights to Preston Public, you know that her flaws are what make her different. You drive around the corner of King and Fountain and breathe deep the brimstone on which she was built.

There, on that fragrant corner of King and Fountain, stands an imposing five-storey building crowned with a garish, red steel roof. Row after row of windows stud the tan stucco façade, and a green, two-storey balcony looms over the impressive front doors. This is Preston Springs, a hotel that has watched over Preston for close to 125 years. It, and the sulfur springs welling through the shale in its basement, built Preston's early reputation as a premier vacation destination. But nobody would stake the town's reputation on the Preston Springs today. The hotel at King and Fountain is derelict, abandoned and rumoured to be haunted, a remnant from better times when Preston was the place to visit and not simply another stop on the way to Kitchener or Waterloo.

According to a hotel brochure from the 1920s—back when the hotel was called the Preston Springs Hotel & Mineral Baths—the abandoned building at King and Fountain was "a beautiful four storey brick and stucco structure, with all the modern conveniences and comforts of the largest city hotel."

The hotel was accessible by train. This railway line now carries cars to the Cambridge Toyota plant and steel to the Babcock & Wilcox industrial boiler factory, Cambridge's two major employers.

The brochure extols the beauty of the surrounding countryside:

> The properties composing The Preston Springs occupy a spot whose altitude commands a view for miles in every direction.
>
> Vistas of unsurpassed beauty present themselves on every hand—here, the quiet waters of the river Speed wind gently through meadows carpeted in softest green; there, a heavily wooded knoll stands out in bold relief against the bright blue of the sky. Everywhere are scenes which would inspire the brush of an artist.

A black-and-white image shows an idyllic tea garden ringed with evergreens. Whitewashed patio chairs sit on a manicured lawn, mottled with sunlight. Tables lounge beneath bright umbrellas.

The hotel featured a spacious rotunda, furnished with "deep Chinese blue rugs," "softly upholstered armchairs," writing desks, board games and a magnificent stone fireplace. The guest rooms were decorated with "delicately coloured chintz," fresh linens and polished wooden furniture.

The Preston Springs Hotel boasted six acres of terraces, tennis courts and bowling greens, magnificent old trees and flagstone walking paths. Guests could visit the Waterloo County Golf and Country Club for dinner and spend the day at Puslinch Lake.

The Preston Springs Hotel was also a sanitarium. Guests could have their ailments diagnosed and treated with healing waters. One striking image in the brochure shows a naked man surrounded by a curious apparatus designed to spray him with water from the underground springs. He faces the wall. Eight brass nozzles poke from the walls, four on either side of the man. Above his head a larger nozzle points directly down; small square drains perforate the floor. To the man's right stands a cabinet and a small table for his belongings. In the foreground, an orderly in white scrubs bends over a countertop jeweled with buttons and levers.

This was all part of the treatment provided by the Preston Springs, a full-service health club that even offered dental surgery and electro-shock therapy. In fact, the Preston Springs was purportedly one of the best sanitariums in the world. Says the brochure:

> A resort therefore, such as The Preston Springs, [...] combines all the comforts and conveniences of the most modern hotel, with the medical facilities of the most efficient hospital [...] the resort is built about one of the most wonderful mineral springs on this continent.

One curious thing in the brochure: guests were encouraged to drink the sulfurous spring water. It was served as an option at dinner.

~~~

The story of the Preston Springs Hotel begins with Peter Erb. The year was 1838. Erb, eighteen years old and eager to find salt, was digging into the rocky soil of the countryside when the air filled with an acrid odour. Peering into his hole, Erb saw the soil was damp. He dug deeper, out of morbid curiosity, and soon a little spring welled up. Thinking the stinky water was not worth his time and effort, he abandoned the spring and returned home to Waterloo.

This marked the beginning of what became Preston. Erb Street in nearby Waterloo is named after this intrepid hole-digger.

Two years later, Daniel Hagey purchased the land, including the spring. He dug deeper and used the spring to drive the overshot wheel in his wagon-making shop. Ten years later, Hagey sold the shop to Samuel Cornell, who built a bathhouse with a boiler and offered hot and cold baths to visitors. Twenty-one years later, in 1871, Christopher Kress purchased the building and renamed it the Hotel Kress. He enlarged and renovated the structure.

In 1890, local businessman Robert Walden built the Del Monte Hotel next door to the Hotel Kress. People flocked to the Del Monte for the fresh air and country vistas. Around this time, Preston's population, comprised mainly of German immigrants, surpassed 2,000.

In the 1920s tourism to Preston dipped. The struggling hotel was sold to brothers Dr. Gordon and Dr. Edwin Haigmeier, who renamed the Del Monte as the Preston Springs Hotel. Celebrities who went to "take the waters" at the hotel included Lord Stanley, the Governor General of Canada from 1888 to 1893 and namesake of the Stanley Cup; Lucy Maud Montgomery, author of the Anne of Green Gables books; and Babe Ruth, the legendary baseball player. Nothing good lasts. Neither did the Preston Springs Hotel. The business floundered.

In 1942, the Royal Canadian Navy purchased the hotel to use as a residence for members of the HMCS Conestoga in Galt, the first Women's Royal Canadian Naval Service training centre.

After the Second World War, the hotel operated as a luxury barracks for female factory workers of a nearby rubber factory.

The old hotel changed hands again in the 1970s. A man named Alan Hodge purchased the building and re-opened the hotel as the Preston Springs Gardens Retirement Home. Hodge took care of the old building, but not the retirement home's residents. In 1990, the city shut down the retirement home for violating the health and safety of residents. That same year, bulldozers demolished the Hotel Kress across the street.

In the years that followed, the old hotel sat vacant. Hodge watched over the building at night from his car, but he couldn't watch every night, and vandals stripped the interior bare.

Today, the building is filled with the remnants of abandoned renovation projects, attempted in 1999, 2006 and 2012. Locals say ghosts of abused and neglected retirement residents haunt the forgotten building and prevent anybody from reviving the building.

Whether anybody can revive the hotel is a question Preston has been asking for twenty-six years.

Maybe the old hotel is haunted. Or maybe it's cursed.

~~~

On our way out of Cambridge to Kitchener, via the route known as Shantz Hill, my buddy's truck rattles down King Street. We pass the old Knox Presbyterian, the Tool Shop and the CIBC, Tommy's Pizza and KFC. We pass that new retirement high-rise and bump over the tracks around the bend to pass the Dempster's flour mill and the old Coffee Time with windows covered with cardboard and FOR LEASE signs. We creak to a stop at the corner, behind a maroon 1999 Grand Am with rust bubbling the edges of the trunk. The sulphur smells strongest at this intersection. A few years ago, a kid died skateboarding when his wheel bit a rock and he fell into traffic beside the Preston Springs.

The hotel looks somewhat like the Southworks building in Galt, an outlet mall inside an old former factory, and a little like Len's Mills, a discount clothing and craft store in Hespeler in a building that was once a textile mill. All three buildings have broad, four-storey tall stone facades studded with windows. All three buildings are ratty and run-down, but the old buildings in Galt and Hespeler, Southworks and Len's Mill are still livable, usable structures that have found new purpose and have grown with their communities. The Preston Springs has been rotting for decades while Preston has grown around the hotel like a tree around a nail.

Why hasn't Preston Springs reclaimed its former glory?

Is it because Preston's centre of town has shifted away from the area? Riverside Park and Preston's downtown haven't moved, but many people now go to the Cambridge Centre Mall to shop. Kitchener-bound traffic continues to motor past the hotel. Nobody stops because there is nowhere to park. Years ago, Paul De Haas, the hotel's current owner, purchased nearby houses to use as parking spaces. But those homes have yet to be torn down and turned into parking spots.

What happened to the beautiful six-acre property featured in those brochures printed in the 1920s? Over the years, the land was portioned off and sold. Now the building is surrounded by suburban neighbourhoods and shopping malls. The Cambridge Centre Mall, a ten-minute drive from the hotel, opened in 1973 and contributed to the town's eastward sprawl away from the hotel. The mall added another 300,000 sq. ft. of retail space in 1990, the same year Preston Springs Gardens Retirement Home was shut down. Did the mall kill Preston Springs?

~~~

Not long ago, an urban explorer trespassed through the old hotel and posted his adventure on YouTube. The video shows signs of redevelopment: ripped out fixtures, torn up flooring, new drywall. But no serious structural re-engineering is happening.

In a YouTube video, Aaron Giesbrecht takes shaky steps along Fountain Street. He points the camera crookedly up at the imposing belvedere. Still images of the interior show a dusty stone fireplace with floorboards stacked nearby and a dark, twisted hallway lined with doorways.

I'm reminded of the thirty residents who lived there after the home went into receivership in 1990. One concerned man went to Queen's Park about the crisis at the retirement home. The legislative records show that from March 19 to 29, residents were without food or heat, except for what meals the home's staff volunteered to bring.

Dave Cooke, an opposition MPP, demanded to know what provincial legislators intended to do about the crisis. Gilles Morin, the minister responsible for Senior Citizen Affairs, replied:

> I am appalled to hear that seniors may have been left with inadequate food and heat for a period of ten days and that none of the appropriate local officials was notified.
>
> Let me tell members what I did. As soon as I found out about this situation, my staff immediately, this morning, contacted local officials, including the placement co-ordination service and the medical officer of health, and put all appropriate people in touch with one another.
>
> I want to assure you that every resident of Preston Springs Gardens Retirement Home will be properly cared for and will have food and heat. Representatives of the receiver, Touche Ross, met with the administrator of the home today to discuss the future of the home. I have been advised that the receiver plans to keep the home open.

Whatever plans Hodge had to keep the retirement home open were never realized. The hotel has been abandoned since 1990.

Giesbrecht walks past the oak banister I've read so much about. Forty years ago, Alan Hodge polished that banister twice a year with linseed oil. It has long since lost its luster. I think of the many nights Hodge spent in his car, watching the building, defending the abandoned structure from vandals. One dark webpage that hosts stories of haunted Ontario buildings tells of the night Hodge saw a light shining on the fourth floor. When Hodge went up, expecting to meet teenage hooligans, he felt a mysterious force push him down the stairs. As he lay at the foot of the stairs, he claimed to have seen a man grinning down at him. The man's torso was "see-through."

Another blogger who explored the abandoned building recounts how a light switch swung down and smacked him in the head just as he entered the building. The brave investigator found no explanation for the attack, no place from which the switch could have fallen.

Giesbrecht directs his camera down the hallway, swinging abruptly into one of the rooms. Daylight illuminates torn, floral wallpaper and exposed lathe. The wooden subfloor is caked with plaster dust. Light shines between the framing timbers into other rooms. All along the walls, dark shadows peer from splintered cavities behind the lathe. The shower stalls have been torn out and piled inside the empty elevator shaft. Building materials—dry wall and steel studs—long since written off, wait in the middle of rooms. The violence of the demolition contrasts with the eerie stillness. The building is so large you wouldn't know if you were alone.

~~~

Simmering

Wet gusts of wind buffet my body as I make my way across Fountain Street on February 10, 2015. This winter has been mild, but temperate days can turn temperamental, and every February rainstorm carries the threat of real, biting winter.

The building looms over me. On its right side, the original hotel structure, a deep balcony stretches over the arched front doors; stone piers anchor the timber beams. On its left extends an off-kilter addition, almost as large as the original building.

Weathered plywood cover the ground-floor windows. The upper windows gaze blackly out over the intersection. As the traffic lights change, the hotel is bathed first in red light, then amber, then unearthly green. I shiver and wrench my eyes away from the windows and study the hotel's gloom for movement. From here, at the foot of the hotel, the ghost stories certainly feel real. But I prefer to believe that the geographical and political growth of Cambridge caused the demise of this place.

I prefer to believe the stories of hauntings are only stories. But as I stride back up King Street in the gathering dark of a cold February evening, I dare not glance back toward those rows of eastward-facing windows. There must be a reason for the failure of this once famous hotel.

~~~

The problem, I learn, is parking. It's been parking all along.

I spoke to Donna Reid, Cambridge City Councillor, Ward 1. She told me that the Preston Springs is a valuable heritage building and that her constituents, the residents of Preston, are worried "something may happen to it." I asked her if she thinks a huge abandoned building affects the character and value of Cambridge's downtown.

16

Isaac Maw

"Well, I wouldn't say abandoned," she says. "The building is vacant, yes. But developers have been looking very closely at it."

I ask what she thinks the cause of its twenty-six-year vacancy might be.

"Parking," she tells me. "There is a parking issue."

In the beginning, the Del Monte Hotel sat on acres and acres of land. Expansive greenspace, good for tea gardens and horseback riding, drew visitors to the hotel. Over the years as Cambridge grew, the original property was carved off and sold.

In an interview with CTV Kitchener in late 2012, Hodge, the previous owner, said, "It's a gracious old building. Something should be done with it. It's got a lot of potential." A month before that interview, Karl Innanen, the listing broker selling the property for Guelph Financial Corporation after the building fell into receivership, said: "As a long-time resident of Cambridge, I am happy to see the process for redevelopment of this great building moving forward. Cambridge's current revitalization efforts in its downtown cores will make this an attractive opportunity for many developers. Like most people, I'm eager to see what evolves from this sale."

In 2012, Innanen sold the property for just under the asking price of $1.29-million to Paul de Haas of the Toronto-based Haastown Group. "There's an opportunity here. There's an opportunity for the city to see this building come back to life," de Haas told *The Cambridge Times*. Soon after he purchased the building, de Haas began redevelopment of the site, but halted for re-evaluation. In March 2014, he relisted the site for double the price he had paid— $2.7-million. He purchased two adjacent residential properties to add to the property. "We're not stopping the work that we would otherwise be doing if we were going to complete the project on our

17

own," he told the *Times*. "Hopefully we find that right group and there's a deal that makes sense for everybody."

In August 2015, the sale listing expired, and de Haas' company is now developing the site on their own. "We've already solved one of the property's biggest challenges by buying the property next door, so we've resolved the parking issue," he said.

Preston Councillor Mike Mann added: "This building is an incredible landmark for Preston. Whenever you leave town or come into town by way of King Street, you see this incredible building—the landmark of our community."

I ask Donna Reid if she thinks there could be any other issue holding the Preston Springs back.

"No, it was really just the parking," she tells me.

~~~

I learn there is, in fact, more to the story than just parking.

According to his website, realtor Faisal Susiwala is the eighteenth best REMAX realtor in the world, top ten in Canada and "#1" in Waterloo Region. His grinning face peers from the grime-encrusted rear-end of Grand River Transit buses all around Cambridge. He's something of a local celebrity. When he was eighteen and attending Galt Collegiate Institute, he sold $2-million worth of properties as a Real Estate Broker. He skipped class to show homes.

Susiwala is interested in Preston's hot spring hotel history. In 2007, he announced a plan with investors from Dubai for a $100-million project to rebuild a historic hotel on the corner of King and Fountain Street.

I was unable to reach Susiwala for comment. He told the local press he wanted to restore the hotel as it was, with a Mansard roof studded with dormer windows, and a large belvedere over the main entrance. "We would move ahead in phases, starting at the front of the property," he said, describing the project for the *Cambridge Times.* "It's an exciting project."

But Susiwala wasn't planning to buy the Preston Springs. He wants to rebuild the Hotel Kress that once stood in the vacant lot across the street from the Preston Springs. Susiwala and his international investors don't think the Preston Springs is worth buying, even if it costs two percent of their budget.

The redevelopment of the Hotel Kress was placed on hold years ago when Cambridge City Council began debating whether to install a roundabout at that corner, which could take a huge bite out of Susiwala's property. Council is still debating the roundabout. Susiwala's Dubai investors have since been replaced with investors from China.

Perhaps Susiwala understands the value of something new.

According to the national census, Cambridge had a population of 126,748 people in 2011. In that year, Preston Springs had been vacant for twenty-one years. For nearly half the residents of Cambridge, the hotel has been nothing but a vacant building since they were in grade school. For nearly a third of the residents, the building has been vacant for their entire lives. Every person who knew the hotel in its heyday, when L.M. Montgomery, Babe Ruth and Lord Stanley visited it, has died.

Cambridge is hardly a place people want to visit—it's more a place to pass through—and over the years, it's become easier to get to Toronto. The Highway 401 was completed in 1964. In 2009, the provincial government established a bus line linking Cambridge to Toronto and Guelph. As for life in Cambridge, the Cambridge

Simmering

Centre Mall, located on the other side of town, far from the Preston Springs, became the city's shopping destination in 1980. Cambridge has grown up without Preston Springs. Nobody needs it anymore.

~~~

Cambridge will grow and change. Faisal Susiwala, all-star realtor, may build his luxury hotel across the street. But the Preston Springs Hotel—protected by its red mansard roof and heritage designation—will keep watch over Preston. And the springs underground will continue to simmer.

Select Chronology

1838   Peter Erb strikes mineral springs in Preston while boring for salt.

1840s   Daniel Hagey uses the spring water to drive an overshot wheel of a wagon-making shop.

1850s   Samuel Cornell builds a hotel on land near the spring. He builds a bath house with a boiler and offers hot and cold baths.

1871   Christopher Kress purchases the building. He renames it the Hotel Kress and enlarges and renovates it.

1890s   The Del Monte Hotel described in a marketing brochure from the late 1890s as a "beautiful four storey brick and stucco structure, with all the modern conveniences and comforts of the largest city hotel," is built next to the Hotel Kress.

1920   Business slows with The Great War and doctors Gordon and Edwin Haigmeier purchase the hotel. They rename it Preston Springs and turn it into a sanitarium and spa.

1942-5 The building is used as a rest home for naval veterans.

1960s? The building may have housed luxury barracks for female rubber factory workers.

1970   Alan Hodge takes ownership of the Preston Springs Retirement Home. Twice a year, he rubs linseed oil on the oak beams throughout the building.

1990	The Hotel sits vacant when "fire safety issues" shut down the Preston Springs Gardens Retirement home.
1990s	Scavengers and vandals slowly gut the building of anything of value. Rumour has it that the building is haunted.
1999	A restoration project begins, but the hotel falls again into receivership.
2006	The building is bought by a King City Corporation.
2007	To present: The city's plans for a roundabout stymy realtor Faisal Susiwala's plans to rebuild the Hotel Kress on the vacant lot where it once stood.
2012	Haastown Developers purchases the building and explores options for redevelopment. They purchase two adjacent homes to expand the property, already spanning 2.5 acres. "Parking will drive this project," says project manager Rob Gazzola.
2014	Preston Springs redevelopment is placed on hold. Haastown Developers look for partners or buyers for the property.
2015	Haastown Developers' sale contract expires and they plan to move forward with the development themselves.

References

City of Cambridge. (n.d.). *House Hansard* (Canada, Ontario Legislative Assembly). Retrieved from http://hansardindex.ontla.on.ca/hansardeissue/34-2/l008_90.htm

City of Cambridge. (n.d.). Evolution of Preston. Retrieved from http://www.cambridge.ca/city_clerk/cambridge_archives_and_records_centre/evolution_of_preston

CTV Kitchener. (2014, March 06). Preston Springs Hotel back on the market at double previous price. Retrieved from http://kitchener.ctvnews.ca/preston-springs-hotel-back-on-the-market-at-double-previous-price-1.1717692

CTV Kitchener. (2014, November 10). Preston Springs Hotel Redevelopment. Retrieved from http://www.waterlooregionconnected.com/showthread.php?tid=277

D. L. (2001-2016). Waterloo Region Generations: Christopher Kress. Retrieved from http://generations.regionofwaterloo.ca/getperson.php?personID=I40567&tree=generations

Durham West Arts Centre. (2007). Women and War: Olive Henderson Womens Royal Canadian Navy Services - Leading Wren No. 210. Retrieved from http://www.readingandremembrance.ca/forms/RR2007/OliveHenderson.pdf

Giesbrecht, A. (Director). (2012). *Preston Springs Hotel: Restless Abandoned* [Motion picture on Youtube.com]. Canada.

Martin, R. (2014, February 08). Preston Springs Redevelopment on Hold. Retrieved from http://www.cambridgetimes.ca/news-story/4357380-preston-springs-redevelopment-on-hold/

Martin, R. (2015, July 30). Redevelopment of Preston Springs Going Ahead. Retrieved from http://www.cambridgetimes.ca/news-story/5766553-redevelopment-of-preston-springs-going-ahead/

Morin, G. (1990, March 29). "Preston Springs Gardens Retirement Home." Ontario. Legislative Assembly. 34th Parliament, 2nd session. Retrieved from http://hansardindex.ontla.on.ca/hansardeissue/34-2/l008_90.htm

Ontario Ghosts and Hauntings Research Society. (1997-2016). Preston - An Old Hotel. Retrieved from http://www.torontoghosts.org/index.php?/20080820354/South-Western-Ontario/Preston-An-Old-Hotel.html

Preston Springs Hotel. (2016). Retrieved from http://www.pandb.ca/preston-springs-hotel/

Reid, D., City Councillor Ward 1. (2016, March 06). About the Preston Springs [Telephone interview].

"Preston Springs Hotel & Mineral Baths" [Brochure]. Retrieved from http://goo.gl/ERW149

Waterloo Region Record. (2011, October 19). Realtor proposes $100-million project. Retrieved from http://www.cambridgetimes.ca/news-story/3375522-realtor-proposes-100-million-project/

Waterloo Region Record. (2012, December 08). Preston Springs Hotel: Historic jewel awaits new owner, new vision. Retrieved from http://www.therecord.com/news-story/2618063-preston-springs-hotel-historic-jewel-awaits-new-owner-new-vision/

Waterloo Region Record. (2012, December 19). Iconic Preston Springs building has a buyer. Retrieved from http://www.therecord.com/news-story/2618137-iconic-preston-springs-building-has-a-buyer/

SEVEN TINY STORIES ABOUT MISSISSAUGA

Cory Song

When I first began this project, I had little faith that Mississauga, the suburb where I was living, could interest me. But as I quickly found out, Mississauga has more stories to tell than I have time to write. These ten tiny stories give a glimpse of the richness of the history of Mississauga. More stories are buried in the old farmlands just waiting to be re-discovered.

1. The First Purchase

In the early 1600s, a group of French traders encountered people living around the North Shore of Lake Huron. These people—the Ojibwa people, closely related to the Algonquin—called themselves the Mississaugas, meaning "River of the North of Many Mouths." By the early 1700s, the Mississaugas lived on the lands around the Burlington Bay, Etobicoke Creek and a river named after the relationship between the Indigenous and European peoples—the Credit.

27

On August 2, 1805, at the Government Inn on the east bank of the Credit, the Mississaugas sold 70,784 acres of land from the Etobicoke Creek to Burlington Bay to the British government. This "first purchase" created the Toronto Township, which opened for settlement in 1806. Between the first purchase and 1847, when the Mississauga people were relocated to the Six Nations Reserve on the Grand River, the Crown acquired an additional 600,000 acres of land from the Indigenous peoples. The Crown sold this land to private landowners, who developed the area into what is today the Region of Peel.

Once the Toronto Township opened for settlement, small villages and hamlets formed to take advantage of the forestry resources. The village of Dixie, originally called Sydenham, formed when settlers began arriving in 1806. Originally home to many Irish Catholics who planted gardens along the Dundas Highway, Dixie became known as an agricultural center. The Clarkson settlement, beginning in 1807, once the "Strawberry Capital of Ontario," was named after Warren Clarkson, who owned the land on which a railway station was built in 1855. Cooksville, first called Harrisville, sat at the intersection of two important roads, Dundas and Hurontario, and became a hub of commercial activity early in the life of the township. Many emerging communities, like the villages of Lakeview and Lorne Park, flourished. Others, like Burnhamthorpe, Sheridan, and Britannia, have since disappeared. Of these lost townships, we remember only their names.

2. The Little Towns Grow

The "second purchase" of October 28, 1818, led to the founding of Meadowvale and Malton. An entrepreneur named Timothy Street attracted settlers to the northern portion of the Toronto Township in the early 1820s with his business and mining ventures. The town that sprang up around his businesses became known as Streetsville.

Erindale, founded in 1820, went through a series of names— Toronto, Credit, Springfield and Springfield-on-the-Credit—before Reverend James Magrath, an early influential settler, lent the name of his estate to the town.

Port Credit, near the mouth of the Credit River, was first surveyed in 1834. Immigrants began to settle there in that year, and the area experienced many economic booms with the arrival of large industry, like the St. Lawrence Starch Company in 1889. In 1863, Frederick Chase Capreol built the first lighthouse at Port Credit.

The 1950s brought significant industry to the township, like the A.V. Roe Aircraft Company in Malton, Hand Fireworks in Dixie and the Petro Canada Oil Refinery in Clarkson. During the 1960s, Xerox built their international headquarters in Clarkson, just north of Port Credit, on an industrial research strip near the QEW highway. IMAX developed its cinematic technology on the same industrial strip. There was even a nuclear research facility nearby.

3. How Mississauga Got Its Name

In 1968, a provincial decree formally amalgamated many of the villages in the Toronto Township. The new town couldn't keep the name "Toronto Township" without putting it forever in the shadow of the metropolis to the east. For Robert Speck, the forty-second reeve of the old town of Cooksville, the newly-established town needed a name before anything else.

Speck had first proposed a new name for the Toronto Township in 1962, six years before the amalgamation. He and many on the council, including a future mayor Ron Searle, favoured the name "Mississauga." But not everybody liked it. Charles "Chic" Myron Murray proposed calling the new town "Sheridan," after one of the townships that had occupied a corner of the old township. In the interest of fairness, the councilors decided to hold a plebiscite to decide whether to name the town Mississauga or Sheridan.

As the councilors prepared to take the question to the residents, a newspaper operating out of a hut in Clarkson exerted an influence that not even its founder, Kenneth G. Armstrong, could have expected.

Armstrong had arrived in Clarkson in 1948 and founded the *Clarkson Lorne Park News*. He partnered with a public relations firm based in Toronto and let the columnists manage the day-to-day operations of the newspaper. The paper quickly folded.

Not wanting to give up on newspapers, Armstrong founded another in 1965 out of "The Cottage," a one room building on the northeast corner of Lakeshore and Meadow Wood Roads.

Armstrong originally planned on calling the paper *Whiteoaks News*, after Whiteoaks, a nickname for the Clarkson area, but Don Edwards, a reporter, photographer and paper deliverer at times, suggested that Armstrong name the paper after the Mississaugas who had originally lived in the area. The newspaper didn't have a name until Speck, a good friend to Armstrong, told him about the upcoming plebiscite. Armstrong named his paper *The Mississauga News*.

In an article from the June 29, 1977 edition of *The Mississauga News*, Armstrong recounts how he settled on a name for the paper:

> Bob Speck told me he thought there was going to be a plebiscite
> on what to name Toronto Township when it was given town
> status by the Ontario Municipal Board [...] There are a lot of

names, but Mississauga and Sheridan were the two leaders. He told me he thought Mississauga had the edge so that's the name we chose to call the paper. We sort of snuck in there before anyone else.

"The South Peel's Brightest Weekly Newspaper," as the paper fancied itself, published its first edition on June 23, 1965. The front page story reported on Reeve Speck's application for town status under the headline "FORESEE MAJOR CITY HERE." Despite going up against two publication giants at the time, *The Streetsville Review* and *The South Peel Weekly*, and despite starting with only eight employees, *The Mississauga News* thrived and remains the only newspaper from 1960s still publishing today.

On December 7, 1967, during municipal elections, the town held the plebiscite, and the citizens chose to name their town Mississauga by a three-to-one margin (11,796 to 4,331). When the Town of Mississauga was founded on January 1, 1968, Armstrong changed his paper's slogan to "The Newspaper a Town was Named After."

4. Square One and Old City Hall

Bruce McLaughlin had a vision. In the late 1960s, his development company purchased a seventy-five-acre plot of farmland near Burnhampthorpe and Highway 10 with the intention of "bring[ing] green space back into urban development." His plan was to build a shopping mall.

Originally named "Green Field Shopping Centre," McLaughlin planned on surrounding his new shopping mall with green lawns meant to evoke the farmlands of old Mississauga. When it was decided in 1972 that "Green Field" needed a new name, McLaughlin remarked how they were "back to Square One"—which is how the mall was named. Square One proved an appropriate name, as the 1.5 million square feet of floor space and acres of parking lots evoke sharp-edged modernity more than they do soft, rolling hills. Square One was the largest enclosed shopping mall in Canada when it opened October 3, 1973.

On June 16, 1969, a fire broke out that almost destroyed the town hall at Confederation Square in Cooksville. Following the fire, McLaughlin convinced town council to move the town hall to the plot of land adjacent to the $44 million shopping center he was building. According to *The Mississauga News*, McLaughlin sold the town a five-storey brown brick building on the northwest corner of Hurontario Street and City Centre Drive and the ten acres of land around it for one dollar.

In 1970, when construction of the new town hall began, council chose to honour its first mayor, Robert Speck, by naming the civic square after him. They held a ceremony to commemorate the day, and Speck planted a time capsule containing town memorabilia in the concrete footings of the new town hall. Council took residency in July 1971. McLaughlin presented the key to the building to Speck at the first council meeting held on Friday, September 10, 1971.

The next year, Robert Speck died of heart problems. In 1977, for the fifth anniversary of his passing, Mayor Ron Searle rededicated the Civic Square in Speck's memory. Speck's family planted a tree.

Said *The Streetsville Review* on July 11, 1977: "The name Robert Speck is forever enshrined in Mississauga following a ceremony dedicating Civic Square to the memory of the former mayor."

Ten years later, Mississauga City Council moved its operations into the $59.5 million building it still uses today. In 1990, the city approved plans for an office tower on the space where the Robert

Speck Civic Square stood. The square was demolished. The tree the Speck family planted disappeared during the construction. The time capsule Speck had buried in the old town hall was never recovered. Today, a short road connects Square One to Hurontario. It is named Robert Speck Parkway in memory of the city's first mayor.

5. Too Big to Be a Town

Mississauga grew quickly. By 1970, an assessment valued Mississauga at $1.85 billion with a population of more than 130,000— too big to be a town. On New Year's Day 1974, the Town of Mississauga— now home to more than 200,000 people and already the twelfth largest municipality in Canada—became the City of Mississauga.

The city had wealth, people and potential. All it needed was an identity.

The new council—including future mayors Ron Searle and Hazel McCallion—set to work by holding a design contest for the newly incorporated city's crest. One hundred and sixty-five people submitted ideas. The winning crest captured how the city wanted to see itself—as respectful of the past and excited for the future. This sentiment was enshrined in the city's motto from 1979: "Pride in our Past – Faith in our Future."

The city crest features symbols of the smaller towns that had been amalgamated into Mississauga. The wings on the crest represent Malton's aviation industry; the water wheel pays tribute to Streetsville's milling tradition; the lighthouse signifies Port Credit; the stalk of wheat remembers the area's agricultural roots.

The city's coat of arms features other important symbols, like the Englishman and the Mississauga chief flanking the shield, the crown of maple leaves and trilliums representing the once unique industrial research strip, with the hydrogen molecule memorializing the nuclear research facility that had been located near the QEW Expressway.

Martin Lyon Dobkin, the newly incorporated city's first mayor, ushered in this vision. Elected on October 31, 1973, Dobkin, a thirty-one-year-old doctor with no political experience, beat the incumbent Chic Murray, who had served the township for sixteen years. Dobkin's winning platform promised a "livable Mississauga" with improvements in transportation, better recreation facilities and improved citizen participation.

During his tenure as mayor, Dobkin acquired environmentally sensitive lands and designated them as public parks. He also sought to expand Mississauga's industrial base by creating a more business-friendly ratio of industrial land to residential land. In Metro Toronto, every acre of industrial land had to be matched with four acres of residential land. Mississauga established a one-to-two ratio.

In 1959, around 57,000 people lived in Mississauga. Soon after it incorporated as a city, nearly a quarter million people lived in Mississauga. By 2017, Mississauga had grown to become the most populous suburb in Anglo-America and the sixth largest municipality in Canada, with more than 700,000 residents. Some people who have lived in the city their entire lives still reside in their ancestral homes. People in their eighties, who once drove a horse and buggy down the same streets where today thousands of cars drive, farmed for a living five minutes away from where the gigantic Amazon warehouse now stands.

6. The Train Derailment

> "It was the most terrifying moment of our lives. The first ex-
> plosion threw us up in the air, and then we hit the ground.
> When we turned around, I'll never forget the sight. It looked
> like something you'd see from a picture of the atomic bomb...
> We thought we were going to be killed."
>
> —Kathleen Dabors, eyewitness
> account of the train derailment.
> *Toronto Star*, November 6, 1999.

Disaster struck seven minutes before midnight on November 10, 1979. A 106-car Canadian Pacific Railway freight train carrying propane, styrene, chlorine and toluene to the Agincourt marshalling yards in Scarborough derailed at the Mavis Road railway crossing. Six of the twenty-four derailed cars exploded when propane spilled onto the tracks and lit the flammable chemicals.

The three men operating the train—engineer Keith Pruss, train-man Larry Krupa and conductor Ted Nichol—all survived the initial crash. Krupa and Nichol managed to release the air brakes and unhook the twenty-seven-car front section of the train, allowing Pruss to move the rest of the train away from the disaster. Propane tanks scattered by the impact were still exploding when the Peel Regional Police and Mississauga Fire Department arrived at the intersection near Dundas and Mavis.

The chemicals posed the real danger. A ninety-tonne tank of chlorine had ruptured close to unstable propane tanks. If one of the propane tanks exploded, the chlorine, a substance used in chemical warfare, would ignite and release a cloud of deadly chlorine gas over the city.

More than 217,000 people in a 125-kilometer radius had to be evacuated. The first evacuation order, in the Woodlands subdivision close to the accident, was issued at 1:47 AM. More than 1,000 policemen from the Greater Toronto Area patrolled Mississauga neighbourhoods during the second evacuation call at 4:15 am, pounding on doors and leaving yellow X's on homes that had been evacuated. The following morning, more than 1,650 patients convalescing in Mississauga hospitals were transferred to 31 other hospitals that had opened their doors from all over southern Ontario.

Nobody died in the train wreck. Emergency crews patched the damaged chlorine tank. Firefighters used an estimated 432 million gallons of water to clean up the site. An investigation revealed that Car 33 had lost one of its axles, dragging the undercarriage of the car until it left the tracks, taking twenty three other cars with it. Following the disaster, the federal government passed legislation to regulate the transportation of dangerous cargo.

Mayor Hazel McCallion, elected as mayor less than a year before the derailment, won international acclaim for her calm but frank demeanour and her willingness to deliver press updates on-location with an openness that the international press said the public rarely saw in politicians. She became known as "Hurricane Hazel," one of Canada's most decorated and popular politicians. At the time of her retirement in 2014, McCallion had won thirteen consecutive terms as mayor, holding 94 per cent of the popular vote and having won by acclamation three times. Her closest election was her last one, thirty-five years after the train derailment. She won that election by her slimmest margin: just 76 per cent of the popular vote—still a landslide, and proof she was still as popular as when that train fell off the tracks and she stepped forward to speak for her city.

7. Out with the Old Civic Center

In 1979, the same year as the train derailment, Mississauga set out to build a new city hall using funds from the sale of water assets to the province, municipal taxes and the sale of old city hall and surrounding lands. A committee held a national design contest for the new civic centre in 1982. The jury for the competition, headed by architect George Baird, evaluated 246 entries. In a unanimous vote, they chose "A Building for Two Seasons," designed by Toronto firm Jones and Kirkland.

"The site for the new city hall is on the divide between town and country," the firm wrote about their work.

Their winning design features open-air columns, an amphitheater and a jubilee garden dedicated to Queen Victoria. The clock-tower and its steel frame represent parts of a windmill, and the cylindrical council chamber evokes a farm silo. There's a chateau-style great house that sits above the open garden. Tying everything together is a barn shaped building in the middle with huge, sweeping doors. The city hall has no front door and instead asks people to enter through the back, as most people do when they enter a farmhouse.

The ground breaking ceremony for the new civic centre coincided with the city's tenth anniversary on May 8, 1984. A year later, in September, 1985, Mayor Hazel McCallion laid the foundation stone with members of the city council and Ontario's Lieutenant-Governor, John Black Aird.

One controversy dogged the ceremonies. The design of city hall called for pale yellow brick not native to southern Ontario. At the time, Mississauga had two functional brick yards that produced bricks using the red clay found in Mississauga. Rather than buy local, the city chose to import yellow brick from a vendor in the

U.S. Not long after construction of the new city hall began, the Mississauga brickyards went out of business. Residents questioned the decision to buy American rather than support its own industry.

The Civic Centre grand opening took place from July 15 to July 18, 1987, and featured a visit from the Duke and Duchess of York. Every portion of the three-day celebration was meticulously planned, including seating arrangements for the royal guests and councilors, timings for when the Duke and Duchess would tour the new building, directions about which escalator they would ride and even what songs the Emerald Knights Marching Band would play before the royals departed.

Since its unveiling, the building has won architectural awards, accolades and criticism.

In 1992, architect Ihor Stecura told *The Mississauga News* that the building is "a symbol to be a symbol. But it's not a building to be worked in." Mayor Hazel McCallion, who led the construction of the city hall, called the civic centre "unique." "It's what we were looking for. There has been a lot of thought put into it. It's truly a people place." Trevor Brody, a professor of architecture at the University of British Columbia, wrote, "the simplest way to understand Mississauga City Hall is to think of it as an over-scale and slightly racy version of a farmyard, the buildings given urban dress and compressed together, but maintaining of their rural roots." Joseph Chin, writing in *The Mississauga News* in 2013, made his criticism plain: "World's ugliest city hall could be in Mississauga."

Two decades ago, the Civic Centre's clock-tower was the tallest building in the area. Since the condo boom, the building has been lost in an urban landscape. The rural motifs built into the design have been buried by the sweeping wave of modernization.

I moved from Vancouver to study in Mississauga in 2013, and by writing these seven tiny stories, learned more about its history than my own hometown. New faces became regular faces. New routines and bus routes, restaurants and relationships, came and went. Mississauga was never my final destination, but the longer I stayed and the more I learned about this new place, the more it began to feel like home.

Select Chronology

1600s   French traders encounter the Mississaugas.

1805   August 2 – "First Purchase" British Crown buys 70,784 acres of land from the Mississaugas.

1806   Toronto Township opens for settlement. Dixie is founded.

1807   Settlers found Clarkson.

1809   Cooksville is founded.

1818   The "Second Purchase" allows for the founding of Streetsville, Meadowvale and Malton.

1820   Erindale is founded

1834   Port Credit is surveyed and settled.

1967   December 7 – Plebiscite for naming of new city: Mississauga or Sheridan?

1968   January – Township of Toronto becomes Town of Mississauga.

1971   October – Old Civic Centre Opens.

1974   January 1 – Streetsville, Port Credit and Mississauga amalgamated into new City of Mississauga.

1987   The new Civic Centre officially opens.

1990   November 21 – Mississauga tears down the Old Civic Centre.

Sources

Armstrong, K. (1965, June 23). Foresee Major City Here. *The Mississauga News*.

Bickford, T., & Arnell, P. (1984). *Mississauga City Hall: A Canadian Competition*. New York: Rizzoli.

Chin, J. (2013, October 25). World's ugliest city hall could be in Mississauga. *The Mississauga News*.

Canada, Mississauga City Council. (1984). *Civic Centre Ground-Breaking Ceremony: May 8 1984*.

Canada, Mississauga City Council. (1985). *Civic Centre Founding-Stone Ceremony: September 14 1985*.

Canada, Mississauga City Council. (1987). *Civic Centre Tour Route For Their Royal Highnesses The Duke and Duchess of York*.

Canada, Mississauga City Council. (1996). *Facts and Figures on the Mississauga Civic Centre*. Mississauga.

Canada, Mississauga City Council. (1987). *The Mississauga Civic Centre Official Opening July 18 1987 Souvenir Program*.

Clark, B. (1982, September 30). Design picked but no date set for new Mississauga city hall. *Toronto Star*.

Hall Comes Down. (1990, November 21). *The Mississauga News*.

Heritage Mississauga - Business & Industry. (n.d.). Retrieved from http://www.heritagemississauga.com/page/Business-Industry

Seven Tiny Stories About Mississauga

Seven Tiny Stories About Mississauga

Heritage Mississauga - Clarkson. (n.d.). Retrieved from http://www.heritagemississauga.com/page/Clarkson

Heritage Mississauga - Cooksville. (n.d.). Retrieved from http://www.heritagemississauga.com/page/Cooksville

Heritage Mississauga - Dixie. (n.d.). Retrieved from http://www.heritagemississauga.com/page/Dixie

Heritage Mississauga - Erindale. (n.d.). Retrieved from http://www.heritagemississauga.com/page/Erindale

Heritage Mississauga - History. (n.d.). Retrieved from http://www.heritagemississauga.com/page/History

Heritage Mississauga - Lost Villages. (n.d.). Retrieved from http://www.heritagemississauga.com/section/?section=8

Heritage Mississauga - Mississauga Heritage Guide. (n.d.). Retrieved from http://www.heritagemississauga.com/page/Mississauga-Heritage-Guide

Heritage Mississauga - Port Credit. (n.d.). Retrieved from http://www.heritagemississauga.com/page/Port-Credit

Heritage Mississauga - Streetsville. (n.d.). Retrieved from http://www.heritagemississauga.com/page/Streetsville

Heritage Mississauga - The Majestic Credit River. (n.d.). Retrieved from http://www.heritagemississauga.com/page/The-Majestic-Credit-River

Heritage Mississauga - Villages. (n.d.). Retrieved from http://www.heritagemississauga.com/section/?section=7

Hicks, K. A. (2005). *Cooksville: Country to City.* Mississauga, Ont.: Friends of the Mississauga Library System.

History in the Making. (1977, June 29). *The Mississauga News.*

Mitchell, B. (1999, November 6). The Miracle of Mississauga. *Toronto Star.*

Saracino, L. H. (1992, July 12). Avant garde or UGLY: Mississauga architecture - love it or hate it. *The Mississauga News.*

Wilkinson, M. (2017, March 3). Interview with Matthew Wilkinson [Personal interview].

A HISTORY OF THE GRANGE

Shalini Nanayakkara

I t rained the first time I visited The Grange. Built sometime between 1828 and 1833, The Grange sits on a one-acre plot of land at the corner of Dundas Street and Sir Johns Homestead in Mississauga, Ontario. Two chimneys poke out from either side of the teal cottage, and two smaller windows—called dormers—emerge from the roof. The Grange is a ten-minute walk from the University of Toronto at Mississauga, where I study. Just past the fence, west towards UTM on Sir Johns Homestead, sits a line of semi-detached houses.

The Grange, once a summer cottage, serves now as the offices of Heritage Mississauga, a non-for-profit charity organization aiming to conserve local history. Heritage Mississauga runs on donations and funding from the City of Mississauga and operates an in-house museum, manages historic archives, publishes on local history and events, offers internships for students and lends communal spaces for theatre troupes and other organizations.

Most intriguingly, their website's "About Us" page ends with the statement, "Together with the support of community groups, corporations and individuals, Heritage Mississauga will continue to accept the challenge of promoting awareness of the community's most precious non-renewable resource." *Most precious non-renewable resource.* These words stick out to me. Perhaps it is somehow tied to how The Grange, this tiny cottage on a green plot of land right beside a busy street, has survived for more than 180 years.

I enter The Grange through the back door, where an "Open" sign hangs. The foyer, which I later learned had been The Grange's summer kitchen, is square and brightly lit by the large windows, with an arching ceiling and a fireplace. The lady sitting at the reception desk greets me. I tell her I have an appointment with Matthew Wilkinson, a historian for Heritage Mississauga. She sends me down a narrow hallway to Wilkinson's turquoise-painted office.

Wilkinson is a big man with a friendly face, receding grey hair and dark beard. He wears a knee brace. A crutch leans against the wall behind a desk situated under a Venetian window.

I shake Wilkinson's hand and he welcomes me to The Grange.

We speak for two hours. Wilkinson introduces me to the first owner of the house, Sir John Beverley Robinson. "That's him over there," Wilkinson says, pointing to a pencil sketch above the fireplace in Wilkinson's office. Sir John regards us with heavy-lidded eyes. His square jaw and tall collar give him an aristocratic air.

And an aristocrat he was. Robinson was, as an article in *Erin Mills Now* describes him, "a political prodigy." Born in Lower Canada in 1791, Robinson was named the Acting Attorney General of Upper Canada at age twenty-two. He went on to become the Chief Justice of Upper Canada and earned his baronetcy in 1854.

In 1821, at the age of thirty, Robinson and another member of the Upper Canada Legislative Council, Samuel Smith, became the "appointed trustees" for 1,628 acres of the 648,000 acres the Crown purchased from the Mississauga "Indians" in 1818. At the time, the area of Mississauga where The Grange stands was called Springfield, and there a village flourished. But five years later, in 1826, Smith died and left Robinson the sole trustee. To finish the job of selling the acreage granted by the Crown, Robinson purchased 100 acres for 200 pounds to build a summer home: The Grange.

Robinson hired the Assistant Survey General of the Province, William Chewett, to construct for him a luxurious Regency-style cottage. Historian Anthony Adamson reports that "[w]hile his neighbours battled encroaching forest, desperately struggling to clear enough land for a crop…and using felled trees for simple log cabins,"

Regency-Style Architecture

The Grange is an example of the "Regency" architectural style that trended in the 1820s and 30s.

Each English architectural design is named after the current monarch—hence we have Elizabethan, Victorian and Georgian. When Mad King George was executed in 1820, England was effectively run under the regency, his son, King George IV.

Known as "The Prince of Pleasure," King George IV hurtled England into debt during his rule.

His "overindulgent" tastes, live on in the "villa-like" French doors, bold colours and wall-encompassing Venetian windows that characterize the Regency style, according to OntarioArchitecture.com.

This style did not lend itself to the cold Upper Canadian winters. Only two or three of the five or six regency structures built in Mississauga remain—and of them, The Grange is the oldest.

Robinson wanted a "playful, elegant small house." But the Chief Justice of Upper Canada forgot one crucial little fact: he lived in Upper Canada.

Adamson surmises that once he began inhabiting The Grange, Robinson found the house cold and drafty. He wasn't the only one. Several later residents of The Grange, including a local doctor named Beaumont Dixie, found the cold penetrating the large windows unbearable. And so, many of the people who lived in The Grange renovated it. Dr. Dixie added an upper story and the summer kitchen. In the 1970s, the Adamsons bricked the exterior for insulation. In 1979, when the City of Mississauga purchased it, the entire house underwent major renovations. By the end of 1981, The Grange had a basement and carpeted floors.

Wilkinson's office was once a dining room. He explains that the wooden floors are fake—that's why they sound hollow—and the walls are painted over. Some nooks still retain the original wallpaper. The bold interior colours, such as the antique primrose yellow in the room opposite Wilkinson's office, reflect what The Grange's exterior colours may have been over the centuries. The Grange had once been burgundy, yellow and its current colour, teal. He adds that during the yellow phase, the cottage was referred to as "The Primrose Cottage."

"We've tried to reclaim the original look as much as possible," Wilkinson says. But with limited government funding, they've had to make compromises and give priority to what's practical. Rolling office chairs don't scratch fake wood flooring as easily as they do real wood flooring.

Cartons of papers and files cover the dining table, fill a cabinet and block off a portion of the floor. These are The Grange's archives.

Wilkinson says he still needs to figure out how to organize these important papers. But first he needs to repaint the peeling bookshelves donated by UTM to The Grange. Wilkinson plans on doing it himself.

"Need to find time to repaint them," he says.

As I leave The Grange, I think about how different the cottage is from contemporary buildings. All around Mississauga is cramped, high-density housing. Government buildings have functional, practical, budget-conscious designs. The Grange is still beautiful. The Venetian windows remind me of ballrooms described in Jane Austen books. Despite the clutter and peeling paint, the office still looks quaint. The cottage's interior is bright and cheery. Its regal exterior is from another time.

The Grange's Famous Owners

The later homeowners didn't renovate The Grange only because of a draft. After Dixie added the upper storey, stables, outbuildings and a summer kitchen, he sold the cottage for 850 pounds with a 120-pound mortgage—more than double what he paid in 1843.

A document from the Brampton Registry Office's Land Registry lists The Grange's owners from the 1830s to 2004. A photocopy of this chart sits on Wilkinson's shelf. The chart, written in an almost illegible cursive hand, also documents The Grange's wildly fluctuating value.

Around 1830, Sir John Beverley Robinson, the Grange's first owner, realized he was going into debt. The British government could not pay for his legislative and judicial work, so Robinson sold the incomplete Grange and fifty acres to Thomas Hickey, a just-married Irish stonemason, for 57.10 pounds—a steal even at the time.

Five years later, Hickey flipped the little cottage to Edgar Neave for 530 pounds.

Neave also built the Benares House, another historic house located south of The Grange in Mississauga. According to the Benares Museum, Neave was a "land developer who profited by selling 'improved' farms to established buyers." A month after he purchased it, Neave sold The Grange at a loss to Colonel William Thompson for 500 pounds. Thompson, who later served as the reeve of Toronto Township, sold The Grange for 400 pounds to Dr. Beaumont Dixie, the famous local doctor. Dixie and his family lived at The Grange from 1843 to 1850, making the cottage a proper family residence for the first time.

The Grange changed hands again on May 18, 1850, when Dixie sold it to John Irvine, who sold it four years later to Colonel Charles Mitchell, the son-in-law of General Peter Adamson, one of the earliest settlers of Springfield and the uncle of the Adamsons, the last family to privately own The Grange. From General Adamson, The Grange exchanged historically insignificant hands until Reverend Henry Grassit, the Dean of St. James's Cathedral in Toronto, purchased the cottage on April 6, 1867. His brief tenancy at The Grange coincides with Canada's year of confederation, a moment marked in the registry by the currency switching from British pounds to Canadian dollars.

In 1892, Weymouth George Schreiber entered the scene. Schreiber and his family owned several homes in Springfield, including Lislehurst, a heritage building on the UTM campus that serves as the residence for the principal of the college. After Weymouth Schreiber passed away in 1910, his wife Charlotte Schreiber, a famous English-Canadian painter, sold The Grange to the Adamsons for

$6,500. The Adamsons, the last private owners of The Grange, sold the property to land developers in 1968 and lived there for another five years as tenants. They sold The Grange for $324,640.

In fifty-eight years, the real estate value of The Grange and its remaining 0.9 acre, pieced away here and there from the original 100 acres, increased almost fifty times over.

How? Land developers needed land to develop what became Mississauga. Why? To answer that question we have to go back to the reason why the British settled here in the first place.

Colonial Real Estate

In the early 1800s, Upper Canada bustled with trade, particularly the trade of land, as the British government had no other way to compensate its middle-upper class officials, like Sir John Robinson. Instead of money, these British citizens were offered land in the colonies, including in Springfield, a village running along Dundas Street West. Springfield was later named Erindale, and finally, Mississauga, after the Indigenous people who had lived in the area.

James Coleman was one such British citizen, who, like many others, regularly exchanged letters with his loved ones on the other side of the Atlantic. He had a wife named Anne and a son named Frank, who just learned to crawl in 1833. Coleman, a doctor, documents this exciting family event in a letter to his sisters back in England. He wrote detailed letters, now typed up and kept in The Grange archives, about life in Upper Canada, while lamenting his homesickness for "dear sweet England."

Amid all of his enthusing over the beautiful Credit River, pickled cabbages and the assembly of fences, Coleman mentions the construction of the cottage opposite of his own land by a certain "Mr.

John Beverley Robinson" in a letter dated 1833. Coleman's letter places the construction of The Grange in the same year.

A transcription of this letter remains in the Heritage Mississauga Archives because it unwittingly disputes the actual date of The Grange's construction. The property receipt in The Grange's archive dates the construction of The Grange as 1828, five years earlier. And according to the land registry, Robinson had already sold to Thomas Hickey by 1833 and purportedly wasn't even in Springfield.

Wilkinson speculates that perhaps Dr. Coleman's letter wasn't received or read by Coleman's sisters in England for five years, though it seems unlikely that cross-Atlantic mail by ship took half a decade. The conundrum of The Grange's actual "birth year" has been debated by many local historians, but none have solved it.

Coleman's letter has created confusion about the date The Grange was constructed, but it also presents a portrait of life in Mississauga in 1833. He describes the village of Springfield as "a rapidly increasing place and one of the prettiest villages in Upper Canada."

> Three years ago it contained only 4 houses, now there are 23 and many more will be erected this summer. There are 4 stores, 2 taverns, a church with a spire and burial ground, a saw mill and grist mill, 2 breweries will commence this autumn. There are now a tailor, a blacksmith, a shoemaker, a cabinet maker, a turning manufactory worked by water and many carpenters and joiners[….] We are a strange mix of nations here, English, Welsh, Scotch, highland Scotch, Irish, Germans, Indians, free Negroes, and Americans and a mixed progeny of the whole of them.

Coleman also mentions a:

> ...tribe of converted Indians at the mouth of the River Credit … These Indians are Chippewas and bear the name of Missisaguas

… There is a tribe of Mohawks not many miles distant … The Mohawks are a much handsomer people than the Missisaguas.

Coleman spends more letter-space on profitable matters, such as how fruitfully Springfield's lands bloom:

We have all the necessities of life in abundance. We have plenty of fruit both wild and cultivated, beautiful wild strawberries as large as the scarlet variety in England and of as fine a flavor. They are to be had in thousands especially on sandy plains and banks. Wild raspberries in abundance, wild plums which make capital pies and puddings, apples and pears are very fine and in very great abundance.

Clearly, the area around Dundas Street West, including The Grange property, has appealed to homeowners for centuries, and not just in the past few decades of suburban mania. Coleman says it best when he remarks, "In no country in the world can money be invested to better account….[i]t is expected that several hundred new houses will be put up in York this summer, which will be an immense place someday or other."

The fruits Coleman loved no longer grow in abundance in what used to be Springfield. The farms have all been carved up and sold to developers, who profit much more from residential buildings than farms—which is exactly how today's Mississauga manifested.

Coleman's own home has long been demolished. In its place, a meat shop called Burton's Meat and Steinway, a piano gallery, stare across a congested Dundas Street at The Grange.

Why Conserve the Past?

"I need these photos scanned by next week," wheezes the woman sitting in front of Matthew Wilkinson's desk. The tiny woman with white cotton candy hair, a knitted peach-coloured scarf and matching knitted beret, wants Wilkinson to scan some old family photos for a magazine article.

It's Februrary 4, 2017, my third visit to The Grange, where I study its historical records. In the dining room-turned-office Wilkinson sits in his chair, his intern Ryan works at the computer desk looking out the large Venetian window and I'm at the square wooden table by the bookshelves. When I arrived earlier that morning, the hefty black folder of The Grange's property records, a notepad and a water bottle awaited me at the table.

I want to thank Wilkinson for his thoughtfulness but he's been dealing with visitors at his desk all day.

First came an artist to hand in—and ask for a critical review of—her artwork for an upcoming exhibition hosted by Heritage Mississauga. She lingered to chat about her work, smiling and giggling. I glanced up at her work. Her landscapes are bright and swirling. Wilkinson told her several times that she's ahead of the game by coming in so early to discuss her displays.

After that, a historian arrived to examine books on architecture tucked in the shelves. She shared my desk with a polite smile and conversed often with Wilkinson.

Then came this woman wanting her photos scanned. She came in from the reception area as soon as the artist left and plunked herself down before Wilkinson's desk.

"I can have these done for you by Thursday, not earlier," Wilkinson says.

"Can't Kevin do it?" she asks.

Having seen only Ryan, and three other female employees in the house, I have no idea who Kevin is.

"Nope, I'm the only one who can do it."

"Well, then. all right. Did you know what happened to Pansy's place?" she says. "Pansy's place. It's all gone now."

I glance up to see Wilkinson's reaction. He does not look up from his computer screen. "Too bad," he replies.

"Mara's is still intact. She sold it to a respectable couple. Educators. But they're going ahead with replacing the windows."

"With what?"

"Something else…that doesn't look as nice."

"Oh well. Probably needed a renovation."

I have no idea how or why Wilkinson is on a first name basis with the acquaintances of this woman, but I'm intrigued. I watch as she stands and puts her peach-coloured knitwear back on. She gives a last, amusing remark, looking at me and over at Ryan with a laughing smile to include us in the joke, before she shuffles out.

I grab Wilkinson's attention before anyone else can distract him. "Busy day, huh?" I say.

"Yeah, yeah," he says. He looks at me tiredly but his smile is cheery as ever.

"Seems like lots of buildings are going down," I say.

"Yeah, to make way for residential areas, mostly. I can't help but wonder how different conservation is going to look a few decades from now."

I exchange glances with Ryan, who listens in on the conversation. He shrugs.

"What do you mean?" I say.

"Oh, the stuff we build our housing with now. Much less solid." And he goes into detail of the solid lumber and brick they used in the past two centuries here in Canada, and how synthetic materials

Cadillac Fairview

Don Mills Development, which later became part of Cadillac Fairview, grew out of business dynamo and horsebreeder E.P. Taylor's development plans for the Don Mills area in 1953.

After World War II, Toronto was "starved" for housing. Taylor turned his eyes towards Erindale, the community that was once called Springfield, after demolishing 20 farm homes and building an 834-hectacre suburb that would "[influence] suburban development for decades."

His proposal—that farmers sell their land and continue life as usual while paying the annual one-dollar rent for life—enticed the Adamsons, the last private owners of The Grange, to sell. Interestingly, Henry Adamson looked after Taylor's horses on his farm.

Taylor retired to the Bahamas, where he continued his land development business. The Canadian Business Hall of Fame describes Taylor as a man who could "always see what most of us couldn't."

now reign. "It's not necessarily built to last, houses today. All these townhouses and condos the development companies are building around Mississauga, they aim to fix the issue of a burgeoning population. In 1957, this area had a population of 59,000. Now it's 740,000. And a lot of it is great, I mean, there's all these students coming to UTM and the like.

"But the buildings they make now are completely different: they're designed to maximize space. And unlike the old days where the guy who builds the place sticks around, we have companies that up and leave when their giant mega-project is done—they don't care what happens to it after it's all built. They don't do repairs. And it's often shocking to see what repairs need to be done on house just a few years old. That's why a little old house like this"—Wilkinson gestures at the walls and ceiling— "can still stand."

"Synthetic housing is most of Mississauga today, isn't it?" I say.

"Yep. But there are a couple farmers kicking around." Wilkinson smiles. "There's a family farther up north—they had a farm not far from here, and they sold their farm for a great price and bought even more land up north. Still kicking."

Once, there were one hundred and fifty-two farms in Mississauga. Today, in 2017, only two farms still operate, past Meadowvale in the north-westernmost part of the city. Most of Mississauga is residential, with endless roads of beige and white housing. The homes just behind The Grange all seem to side-eye the little blue cottage.

Despite the rapid changes in Mississauga, Wilkinson has a positive outlook for the heritage industry.

"Conservation isn't about sealing the past away forever," he says. "It's about growing, growing with the times. It's about always being ready when people come looking for you."

Who Saved The Grange?
When I revisit The Grange on Thursday February 17, 2017, the reception is empty.

I head down the hallway to the turquoise room at the old front entrance of the house. I hurry by the little, mustard-coloured office of Jayme Gaspar, the Executive Director, whispering, "I'm here to see Matthew." I catch Jayme's nod and go on my way. Wilkinson sits in his usual spot, facing his bright-faced computer, and looks up when I breeze in.

"Sorry I'm early," I say breathlessly. I take off my bag and place my coat around the wooden chair, next to the study table near the bookshelves facing the doorway.

"Not at all. You're saving me from this PowerPoint presentation," Wilkinson says, grinning. "It's for the City—a presentation on our proposed activities for the 105th anniversary of the War of 1812. I get five slides and five minutes." He laughs.

"That doesn't seem like much time," I say as I take out my pen and paper.

"No," he agrees. "I'll have to find a way to cram everything in. The City doesn't want to hear anything that 'we hope' to do, only what we have a budget for, but then this presentation is supposed to garner the funding so we can do the stuff we hope to do, so…" He throws his hands up in the air. "Anyway, how can I help?"

"I was wondering," I say. "The Grange started out with 100 acres, and slowly it's been chipped away."

By the fifties, farmers around The Grange had sold their land to development companies. In 1968, Harvey Adamson, the last private owner of The Grange, sold the property to Don Mills Development and leased the place for five years at $1 a year.

Don Mills Development, which became part of Cadillac Fairview a year later, planned to demolish The Grange and use the land for housing.

"Well," I say, "I want to hear about how The Grange was saved."

"As I mentioned in the e-mail," Wilkinson says, "there were many players that stopped them from demolishing the home." The historian cites City Councilor David Culham as one of them, but there were others, including Grant Clarkson, a politician, and Betty Bull, the Director of the Mississauga South Historical Society.

1. David Culham

According to Wilkinson, it was really by "happenstance synergy" that all of these characters converged to save the house, and that the multiple pressures from all sides—municipal, corporate and community—ultimately collapsed Cadillac Fairview's plans to demolish The Grange.

But City Councilor David Culham, who governed the ward in which The Grange sits, and who Wilkinson admits was the main player in that mid-70s war of the wills, thinks otherwise. Mr. Culham believes he catalyzed The Grange's rescue with his intense personal involvement.

"Some people were just amusingly wrong," he told me over the phone. "The reeve at that time tried to take the credit, when in fact he was an actual roadblock in the proceedings."

Culham stated that while the first meeting with Cadillac Fairview and the City over The Grange was "disastrous," his lunch with the land developers at McDonald's afterwards was not.

"The reeve had been too pushy," Culham claimed. "Too boisterous, pushy and bullying. Too much of a politician. So I did it a different way. We went out for lunch and I said, 'listen, you don't want this [property] on your hands.' I understand the corporate pride of not wanting to give up to political pressure. They refused to give it up to the City, but they handed the deed over to me. And not just to the house, but with the one acre too."

They handed it all over because, as Culham said, he "made them look good." Instead of strong-arming the corporation to handing over the land for preservation, Culham claimed that personally appealing to Cadillac Fairview, by painting a picture of "boosting their image to preserve the community" and showing "how they could shape the future," persuaded Cadillac Fairview to sell The Grange to the city.

"I wanted to instate a new philosophy," Culham said. "I would talk mildly in public, and tough behind the scenes—you know, to say, to get things done. Maybe not 'tough' exactly, but honest. Honest and upfront about what needed to get done."

Was Mr. Culham the catalyst for The Grange's rescue? A 1975 article in *Erin Mills Now* appears to think so. The article paints him as the ultimate go-getter, saying that, "Councillor David Culham wanted the house to be preserved and with the cooperation of Cadillac, it was turned over to him to be donated to the City of Mississauga." Culham's influence on Cadillac Fairview's decision appears in several 1970s newspaper articles.

2. Grant Clarkson

Grant Clarkson, another politician involved in saving The Grange, was the Chairman of the Credit Valley Conservation Authority and Vice-Chairman of the Peel County Historical Society. His first love was environmentalism, which expanded to heritage and conservation. He was a founding member of Heritage Mississauga, and as Wilkinson says, a big man with a room-commanding charisma. His high-tier network of politicians and influencers, government somebodies and ground-shakers, had an overarching impact alongside the grassroots sentiment for conservation sprouting from the community. Clarkson passed away in 2011, but he smiles from a 1975 photo of the players involved in the little cottage's rescue. The photo hangs in the entrance of The Grange.

3. Betty Bull

Missing from the photo hanging at the entrance of The Grange is Betty Bull, the Director of the Mississauga South Historical Society. The MSHS was founded in 1963, when people just began to be concerned with historical conservation and heritage in Mississauga.

This concern coincided with the township's 1974 rechristening as "Mississauga" after 74 years of being called Erindale. According to Wilkinson, Bull may have helped to focus the community's concerns into a force advocating for The Grange's preservation.

Bull's advocacy may have been a family affair. According to Wilkinson and the digitized photos he showed me on his computer, Bull's daughter Peggy and her fiancé actually lived in The Grange between 1974 and 1976, in the two years that Cadillac left the cottage boarded up for demolition. Wilkinson says that local newspapers featured this strange event, so the community must have been aware of Peggy's decision and became further intrigued by the charm of this little home.

According to the *Erin Mills Now* article, Cadillac Fairview had allowed tenants to live in The Grange, as long as they didn't alter the property, "in order that every detail of its historic character should be preserved."

But Wilkinson pokes a hole in this reasoning. Apparently, Cadillac Fairview did not allow tenants into every property they owned, especially after the development boom of the 1950s. Wilkinson has not found any records of approval for people to live in The Grange while it was boarded up. Peggy Bull and her fiancé must have squatted at The Grange. The fiancé reportedly articled for Cadillac Fairview, and so an agreement may have been struck off-record.

But there was one issue: the house had been ransacked. No one knows for sure what happened to all the furniture, including a piano, between the Adamsons' departure in 1973 and their brief return a year later. How did Peggy manage to live in the drafty, unfurnished, boarded-up cottage? According to Wilkinson, Peggy's mother collected antique pieces, so perhaps she lent the couple some furniture.

In a photo the blonde-haired Peggy smiles tranquilly, her forearm draped over the footboard of a canopy bed. We can also see a desk, a chair, a dining table and what looks like a chest of drawers in the picture. This squatter lived in relative style.

I reached out to the Mississauga South Historical Society to ask about Mrs. Betty Bull and her daughter's involvement. They responded almost two weeks later that, while eager to help, they had no information about the Bulls. Their archives are all stored in The Grange's attic, and Wilkinson can't access them because he doesn't know how MSHS organizes their archives.

4. A Historian

Wilkinson reckons an expert who understood the "significance of heritage" and had an immense foresight began the long haul to preserve The Grange.

"Was it Culham?" I ask.

"No, no," says Wilkinson. "To say he started the movement...I don't think politicians start the movement to preserve something." Politicians, the historian notes, instead tend to "back the winning horse." Someone, who knew the immense amount of money it would take to repair the "not in great shape" little cottage, with the foresight that The Grange would be in trouble but would be valuable to the cultural preservation of the area, planted the seed long ago.

"Was it Betty Bull? Was it Jean [Adamson]?" Wilkinson muses. Jean Adamson, an avid historian, married Tommy Adamson, a descendant of The Grange's last homeowners. "Jean wrote about The Grange while Harvey [Adamson] was still alive [and living there]." It would be eleven years before Cadillac Fairview granted the deed to the City.

5. The Community
I found convincing evidence of community involvement myself. Tucked away in the three-inch-thick Erindale archival file in the Mississauga Central Library's Canadiana Reading Room are two little community surveys conducted by the Stark Temparale Architects and Planners. Neither survey contains dates, but they mention the City of Mississauga, which dates them post-1974 when Mississauga was incorporated.

These surveys reveal a consensus of the Dundas Street/ Mississauga Road community, and perhaps the Mississauga suburb-city in general, favouring the preservation of The Grange. Forty-five per cent of the surveyors cited the traffic speed and noise on Dundas as a major dislike, while another thirty-five per cent cited overdevelopment. Some recommendations suggest a desire to halt "further development" in the area, "retain low density zoning," "retain and enhance historical aspects" and "retain village image."

In any case, in whatever era this was documented, the people in Erindale have been frustrated for a long time with the thoughtless expansion of land development and would have likely supported, and may have perhaps begun, the fight to preserve The Grange.

6. Cadillac Fairview
"Heritage was in its infancy back then [in the 1970s]," Wilkinson says. The Ontario Heritage Act came into effect only in 1975. Boarded-up houses were a common sight, and so were squatters. In five years, Cadillac Fairview accrued some 4,000 acres of property, which they demolished or left to "sit empty."

Mr. Gerald Sheff, then Vice-President of Cadillac Fairview's New Communities Group, features alongside Culham in every article about the successful transfer of The Grange's deed in 1975. A transcript of Mr. Sheff's remarks concedes that:

> ...rarely do [land developers] take part in an occasion such as this. In effect, we are dealing with the drama of Canada's history and the romance of remembering what this ground on which we now stand was like more than 100 years ago...[and] share this mutual respect we have for our historic past.

Reporters of the time consistently quote Sheff saying similarly inspired sound-bites about preserving the community. In the summer 1975 edition of *Erin Mills Now,* he says, "This building will round out the integrated, fully-planned nature of the Erin Mills community, providing a link with its earliest settlement." In December of 1975 *Mississauga Review* cites Mr. Sheff saying, "Many of the hand-carved mantels, the exterior cornices and the window frames are still original. Our company is delighted to make this building available for the benefit of the citizens of Mississauga."

"Land developers are money-makers [...] They don't give away money," Wilkinson notes. The donation of The Grange was not really a donation at all: the City of Mississauga actually still paid for it, and they paid a hefty amount. "As long as the per capital development dollar stays the same for their acreage," Wilkinson says, "they're still making money." It was a gift in the sense that Cadillac Fairview "didn't have to," but with Mr. Culham's reasoning of reputational capital and the City's money, it wasn't a hard decision.

The historian even speculates that the "higher-density" townhouses on Sir Johns Homestead may have been an agreement struck between the City and Cadillac Fairview, in compensation for loss of profit of not turning The Grange's one acre into residential area, especially the "empty geography" of the lawn.

Wilkinson makes one thing certain. "Projects are in the works long before they make it to documentation," he says. Land-developers never make a split-second decision. This was a calculated move, regardless of Mr. Shreff's waxing on the "romance of remembering."

So who saved The Grange? Savvy people-person David Culham, high-tier Grant Clarkson, community-rousers Betty and Peggy Bull, or the generously self-interested Cadillac Fairview? Was it the people of Erindale at large?

Wilkinson may be right: it was a mix of everyone's involvement. The true preserver of The Grange, and of history as a whole, is the "happenstance synergy" of interested parties wanting to halt our fast-paced world for just a little while longer.

Heritage Site Designation

According to the Canadian Register of Historic Places, The Grange formally became recognized as a heritage site on the September 6, 1977. The Grange was one of the first designated heritage sites in Mississauga after the 1975 Ontario Heritage Act legislation was passed.

This Act allows Municipal Heritage Committees to pass heritage-designating by-laws on any property they consider either an archeological site or "of cultural value or interest" to the current and future community.

According to the Ontario Ministry of Tourism, Culture, and Sport, homeowners of heritage houses enjoy tax breaks. But these tax breaks come with a caveat: As a 2016 *Globe and Mail* article mentions, since the government recognizes these homes for their "soul, character and good bones," any renovations and even repairs must be approved by a city-level committee.

A History of The Grange

Conserving Our Heritage

I explored the land development and heritage issues surrounding The Grange and came out with more human stories than I expected. I found the precious, non-renewable resource that Heritage Mississauga mentions on their website. This resource resides inside the walls of The Grange. It has survived time and industry. It speaks of the flawed but important stories of immigration, settlement, development and making the best out of what's available.

In 1978, the City of Mississauga deliberated on the function of The Grange. Today, Heritage Mississauga has made The Grange everything that the 1978 discussions wanted it to be: a museum, an art gallery, a community space and an office. With new art and history exhibits booked well into 2018, The Grange is lively and busy.

But Wilkinson isn't done. He still has to organize the historical documents filling the crates in his office. He is also unhappy with the pale green paint that colours the hallway—it doesn't work well with either the bright turquoise of Wilkinson's office room or the golden antique primrose of the gallery.

Someday, Wilkinson hopes to get everything up to standard.

The Grange Today

The last document I examine in The Grange's archives is a one-page summary called "Home at The Grange," a work written by Matthew Wilkinson himself. I read it on my computer by lamplight on my bed—it's midnight, but from the get-go I can feel his exuberant presence, as if I am sitting across his desk at The Grange.

"This delightful testimony to life in early years of settlement, The Grange, tells its story through the amazing number of memorable personalities who have owned and occupied it over the years," he begins.

> If only these walls could talk! Seeing the Christmas tree set up in the front room, with the fireplace and mantle, leads me to reflect on Christmas' past. What must Christmas at The Grange have been like for young Richard, Wolstan, Eleanor and Anna Dixie? Were stockings hung with glee on the mantle [...]? [...] Dr. Dixie's children were likely the first children to celebrate Christmas here.

The Grange gains its importance from the people who inhabited it. The four Dixie children—Richard, Wolstan, Eleanor and Anna—died young, but it's through their eyes that this house has value. And to go further, the aristocratic demeanour of John Beverley Robinson, the enterprising eye of Edgar Neave, the benevolent practice of Dr. Dixie, the artistic confidence of Charlotte Schreiber and the stubborn spirit of Peggy Bull, all weave into the non-renewable history living in the walls of this little surviving house. They give The Grange the character that has allowed it to stand after 180 years. It is a site of memories, of heritage, no matter its real estate value.

I read Matthew's little story, smiling at the words of this generous historian with whom I've talked to on many afternoons after class. Wilkinson adds things in this write-up that he never mentioned to me in person, like the names of the Dixie children, though I am sure he would have if we had the time.

I stop when I get to the bottom of the document.

Wilkinson writes that Harry Adamson, the last private owner of The Grange, was his great-great uncle.

In all of the sessions, Wilkinson never once mentioned to me that he was related to the last private owners of the house where he now works. He never mentioned that Harry Adamson's two great-grandsons, who live in Phoenix and Scotland and with whom Wilkinson had met a couple of times over the years, are his cousins.

So I visit The Grange one last time, in April 2017.

Two construction workers saw wooden planks for construction on the sidewalk just in front of The Grange. They stop sawing to let me pass. They clearly hadn't thought that anyone would veer off Dundas Street West onto Sir Johns Homestead to use the sidewalk. Most residents here probably just use their car.

Wilkinson shakes my hand for the final time, cheerier than ever. As if he knew I had read the letter and came seeking answers, he tells me about his great-uncle Tommy Adamson, one of the last children to grow up in The Grange. He shows me a treasure trove of Adamson heirlooms, including a photo of Colonel Peter Adamson's gravestone, which lists all of his battles and displays the Portuguese honorary title he earned in battle, the "Knight of the Towering Sword." Wilkinson also shows me the very Anglican Adamson coat of arms and recites their motto, "Touch not the cat but with a glove." As one of the first settler families, the Adamsons are a pretty big name in Mississauga history, though not to be mistaken for the wealthier Adamsons originally from Port Credit. Wilkinson confides that he's a "giant" compared to everyone in his family—the Adamsons are notoriously short—all the way back to the decorated Colonel. He tells me that his great-uncle Tommy Adamson was a father figure to him.

It may be difficult to explain why people feel the need to conserve local history, but it's not as difficult when it concerns family history. This may be why The Grange still stands today.

Select Chronology

1796 Implied construction of Dundas Street West in the Springfield (Mississauga) area.

1828-33 The Grange was built on 100 acres of given lands. Exact dates are contested, but 1828 is largely held as the year of construction. Sir John Beverley Robinson moves in to use as land sales office and summer home.

1830 October 20. Robinson sells The Grange property to Thomas Hickey.

1833 Dr. James Coleman, Robinson's neighbour, writes to his sister to say that Robinson is ready to start building the house, contradicting the construction date set down in other documents.

1834 The area becomes known as Springfield (also known as Springfield-on-the-Credit) as York turns into Toronto.

1843 The Dixies purchase The Grange.

1840s Dr. Dixie adds the upper story, summer kitchen, and out-buildings. Four of the five Dixie children pass away from illness.

1892 Weymouth and Charlotte Schreiber purchase The Grange.

1900 Springfield-on-the-Credit becomes "Erindale" by popular vote.

1910 Charlotte Schreiber sells to the Adamsons after husband Weymouth's passing.

1920   Henry Adamson adds a brick veneer to The Grange to better withstand the weather.

1960   Heritage Mississauga is founded.

1968   July 30. The Adamsons sell the house to land developers.

1974   Erindale becomes part of the City of Mississauga.

1975   The Ontario Heritage Act is enforced and Cadillac Fairview agrees to donate The Grange.

1977   The Grange becomes one of the first buildings in Mississauga "designated as an architectural and heritage site."

1979-81   The City of Mississauga renovates The Grange.

2004   Heritage Mississauga acquires The Grange from the City.

2005   December 4. Heritage Mississauga officially opens offices at The Grange.

Sources

"145 year old house to be donated to Mississauga." (1975, Summer). *Erin Mills Now.* Retrieved from Mississauga Central Library, Local Archives – Erindale.

"145 year old house to be donated by developers of Erin Mills." (1975, December 13). *Mississauga Review.* Retrieved from Mississauga Central Library, Local Archives – Erindale.

"About Us." (n.d.). Retrieved from http://www.heritagemississauga.com/page/About-Us

Adamson, A. (1978, December 13). "A report on the Robinson-Adamson House formerly called 'The Grange' at Erindale, owned by the City of Mississauga." Retrieved from Mississauga Central Library, Local Archives–Erindale.

Adamson, J. (1969, April 11). "Robinson-Adamson House, Ontario Inventory of Buildings." Retrieved from Mississauga Central Library, Local Archives – Erindale.

Adamson, J. (1978). *Erindale at the crook of The Credit.* Cheltenham: The Boston Mills Press.

"Benares Historic House." (n.d.). Retrieved from http://www5.mississauga.ca/rec&parks/websites/museums/pdfs/benares.pdf.

Bhasin, M. (2015, 12 January). Mississauga's home on the Grange. *The Medium.* Retrieved from https://themedium.ca/features/mississaugas-home-on-the-grange/.

71

Boyd, A. (2016, July 21). "Once upon a city: How Don Mills changed city building." *The Star*. Retrieved from https://www.thestar.com/yourtoronto/once-upon-a-city-archives/2016/07/21/once-upon-a-city-how-don-mills-changed-city-building.html

Brampton Registry Office: Toronto Township Land Abstracts – Lot No. 2 Range 1. (n.d.). Retrieved from Heritage Mississauga, Local History Resource Files.

"Building Styles: Regency (1820 - 1860)." (n.d.). Retrieved from http://www.ontarioarchitecture.com/regency.htm#RegencyDundas.

Coleman, J. (1833). My dear sisters.... Retrieved from Heritage Mississauga, Local History Resource Files [transcribed by Jean Adamson].

Collins, R. (2006, July 12). Life "between the Usk and the Lug." *Booster Newspaper*. Retrieved from Mississauga Central Library, Local Archives – Erindale.

"City takes over oldest building." (1978, October 11). Unknown newspaper. Retrieved from Mississauga Central Library, Local Archives – Erindale.

Case Studies: Erin Mills. (n.d.). Retrieved from https://web.archive.org/web/20081121005929/http://www.condrain.com/archive-cs10.html.

"Designating heritage properties: A guide to municipal designation of individual properties under the Ontario Heritage Act." (2006). Pp. 7. Retrieved from http://www.mtc.gov.on.ca/en/publications/Heritage_Tool_Kit_DHP_Eng.pdf.

E.P. Taylor. (n.d). Retrieved from http://cbhf.ca/ep-taylor.

Erindale. (n.d.). Retrieved from http://www.heritagemississauga. com/page/Erindale.

"Explore Erindale's heritage." (1987, August 5). *The Mississauga News*. Retrieved from Mississauga Central Library, Local Archives – Erindale.

"Fire at Erindale." (1919, May 6). *Toronto Daily Star*. Retrieved from Mississauga Central Library, Local Archives – Erindale..

Fohr, M. (1993). "Erindale: The rise of a village." Retrieved from Mississauga Central Library, Local Archives – Erindale.

Franko, I., & Tardif, J. (1983). The Robinson-Adamson House is truly remarkable. In *Mississauga's heritage: The formative years, 1798-1879*. Mississauga: The City of Mississauga.

Hayes, Derek. (2008). *Historical Atlas of Toronto*. Toronto: Douglas & McInyre Ltd.

Heritage Network. (n.d.). Retrieved from http://www.heritagemis-sissauga.com/page/Heritage-Network.

Heritage Staff. (n.d.). Retrieved from http://www.heritagemissis-sauga.com/page/Heritage-Staff.

Heritage Resource Centre at the Grange. (n.d.). Retrieved from http://www.heritagemississauga.com/page/Heritage-resource-Centre-at-the-Grange.

Hicks, K. A. (2009). *Erindale: Early times to evolution*. Mississauga: The Friends of Mississauga Library System.

Jermyn, D. (2016, August 24). Owning a heritage house brings cost along with the beauty. *The Globe and Mail*. Retrieved from http://www.theglobeandmail.com/report-on-business/owning-a-heritage-house-brings-cost-along-with-the-beauty/article31529767/.

Laiu, Simona. (2004). The Robinson-Adamson Grange: a short history. *Heritage News 17*(4). Retrieved from Mississauga Central Library, Local Archives – Erindale.

Mississauga Growth Forecast.(2010, July). Retrieved from http://www5.mississauga.ca/research_catalogue/F_18_Mississauga%20Growth%20Forecasts%20-%20Population.pdf.

Ontario Heritage Act (n.d.). Retrieved from http://www.mtc.gov.on.ca/en/heritage/heritage_act.shtml.

Dixie Book Part 2 1851-1900–City of Mississauga. Retrieved from http://www.mississauga.ca/file/COM/9635_DixieBook_PartTwo.pdf.

Syed. A. (n.d.). Reverend James Magrath at St. Peter's Historical Plaque. https://localwiki.org/mississauga/Reverend_James_Magrath_at_St._Peter%27s_Historical_Plaque.

Robinson-Adamson House. (n.d.). Retrieved from http://www.historicplaces.ca/en/rep-reg/place-lieu.aspx?id=15498.

Robinson-Adamson House, Heritage Property Database, description and photo. (n.d.). Retrieved from Mississauga Central Library, Local Archives – Erindale.

Spring 1975 – the handling over of the Adamson-Robinson House as a gift by Cadillac Fairview Corporation. [Photograph]. (1975). Retrieved from Matthew Wilkinson, Heritage Mississauga.

Stark, J. B. et al. (n.d.) Erindale village study. Stark Temparale Architects and Planners. Retrieved from Mississauga Central Library, Local Archives – Erindale.

"The Grange: a short history." (n.d.) Retrieved from http://www. heritagemississauga.com/assets/The%20Grange%20 -%20a%20short%20history.pdf.

Two farmers by The Grange barn. [Photograph]. (1910). Retrieved from Matthew Wilkinson, Heritage Mississauga

Weeks, V. M. (1999). *Erindale: The pretty little village.* Mississauga: Verna Mae Weeks.

Welcome to the Grange: The Robinson-Adamson House [Brochure]. (n.d.). Mississauga, ON: Heritage Mississauga.

Weymouth George Schreiber (1826 - 1898). (n.d.). Retrieved from https://www.wikitree.com/wiki/Schreiber-428.

Wilkinson, M. (n.d.). Home on The Grange [Word document].

Wilkinson, M. (2017). Personal communication.

LISLEHURST

Rediscovering a House's History

Jessica Cabral

Part I: The House on the Credit

T he hardwood floor, refinished but original to the 130-year-old house, creaks beneath my boots as I follow Paul Donoghue, University of Toronto Mississauga's Chief Administrative Officer and my personal tour guide, through the empty halls of Lislehurst.

Lislehurst, one of the oldest homes in Mississauga, is located on Principal's Road on University of Toronto property. It is currently vacant. Traditionally, the Vice President and Principal of UTM occupies the house, but Professor Ulrich Krull, the interim principal, has decided against moving into the residence during his interim appointment from September 1, 2016 to August 31, 2017.

In the middle of the main living room, carpets have been rolled up and piled. The room is empty except for a chair by the door. In another room, Charlotte Schreiber's painting "Olivia Paring Apples" hangs over the piano. The painting depicts a young woman holding an apple and a knife and staring absently into the distance.

Donoghue leads me through the kitchen, renovated in 2002 to add marble countertops and stainless steel appliances, through the dining room and the library, and into the ground floor washroom located at the rear of the house. Donoghue laughs as we squeeze into the small powder room occupied by only a sink, a toilet, and a sealed wooden door – the original entrance to the Schreiber family home.

A beige carpet lines the staircase leading upstairs. Plaster carved to resemble individual tiles covers the ceiling. Up the stairs, we weave through vacant bedrooms and into Donoghue's favourite room: a washroom with vibrant teal and orange accented tiles and a walk-in shower. Down the servants' stairs and into the servants' quarters, pine flooring contrasts the oak panelling that adorns the rest of the house – a symbol of privilege for the upper-middle class Victorians who first lived here.

As I breathe in the stale air of this empty manor, Donoghue tells me that of the three original homes Weymouth Schreiber built on this land in 1885, only Lislehurst has survived.

This house is not only the secluded living quarters for University of Toronto Mississauga's principal, but a relic of Erindale's past and a passageway into our campus history. Who was the family that built this house? What was their story? How did U of T come into possession of such a grand property? I have lived in Erindale for my entire life, yet I had never heard of Lislehurst before. Now, as a student at UTM, I want to learn all I can about this little castle of Erindale.

1. Lislehurst's Competing Histories

A range of sources—from nineteenth century newspaper articles, to local histories, to the university archives—chronicle the origin of Lislehurst in a similar way. These sources say the property ended up in the family of Sir Isaac Brock, a British army officer assigned to Canada with his army unit in 1802. The document "History of the Grounds Comprising the New and West Campus of the University of Toronto at Erindale," located in the University of Toronto Mississauga library archives, reports that the Legislature of Upper Canada gifted the land to Brock as a "posthumous recognition of the services which he had performed for the country" during the War of 1812.

Brock lost his life during the war, so his family took ownership of the property. With no apparent use for the 150-acre stretch of land next to the Credit River, the war hero's brother Daniel DeLisle Brock passed the property to a niece, Louisa DeLisle, who lived on Guernsey Island off the coast of Normandy.

Almost identical versions of this story appear in Erindale College's *Lislehurst Tour Notes* from the summer of 1995 and in undated newspaper articles from two unnamed newspapers located in the UTM archives, including "The Schreibers of Local History" and "General Brock's Relatives Sell 40-acre Farm."

However, the story may not be accurate.

Matthew Wilkinson, a historian at Heritage Mississauga, an organization dedicated to preserving Mississauga's history, explains that although there is a loose family connection between the Brocks and the Schreibers, the family that eventually owned the land, no documents directly link Sir Isaac Brock to the property designated Lot 4, Range 3 of the Credit Reserve where Lislehurst now stands.

Lislehurst

The alternate history of Lislehurst says that the Crown patented the property and in 1836 sold it to the Honorable Peter Adamson, the founder of St. Peter's Anglican Church, standing today at the north-east corner of Mississauga Road and Dundas Street. A banker for the Northern Railway Company named Edward Shortiss, who was both a distant relative to Brock and the Schreibers, purchased the lot from Louisa DeLisle in May 1854.

The ownership of the house between Adamson's possession and Shortiss' purchase is unclear; however, Shortiss lost the property to Louisa DeLisle when she foreclosed his mortgage in 1861. Louisa DeLisle remained unmarried and after visiting her relatives in England in 1869 deeded the property to Weymouth Schreiber and his wife Harriet DeLisle's three children, Weymouth George, Herbert Harrie and Edith, as a gift in trust.

Harriet DeLisle died in February 1861, and fourteen years later the widower Schreiber married his cousin, the established English artist Charlotte Mount Brock Schreiber (nee Morrell), who was also a distant cousin of both the DeLisle and Brock families. That year, Weymouth Schreiber, his forty-one-year-old bride and the three children from his first marriage moved from England to Toronto, Canada. In 1885, the Schreiber family constructed a trio of houses on the 150-acre property. The last remaining of those houses is Lislehurst, the private dwelling reserved today for UTM's principal.

In her book *Erindale: At The Crook of The Credit*, Jean Adamson writes that "Mr. Schreiber owned a section of Toronto west of Yonge St. around St. Clair Ave. and Foxbar Rd when it was just fields used as pasture" between 1875 and his move to Springfield-on-the-Credit (later named Erindale) in 1885. The family called their Toronto home DeLisle Ave. until Charlotte renamed it Deer Park.

During the ten years between 1875 and 1885, the Schreiber family built a permanent estate in Toronto, while constructing temporary summer houses in Springfield-on-the-Credit. Schreiber and his family initially used the land as weekend escapes from their bustling lives in Toronto.

The land's inheritance and the connection between the Brock and Schreiber families stirred controversy among citizens in the surrounding areas. Although the issue wasn't publicly expressed during the property's exchange in 1869, in 1905, a curious local sent a question to the local newspaper *The News*, proving that after 36 years the concern for ownership of the property was still town gossip.

The inquiry came from an individual writing under the pseudonym "Sherbourne Street" who wrote:

> Now, as [Sir Isaac Brock] left no direct representatives, I am induced to ask for information respecting his probably nearest collaterals. They may possibly be found in the children and grandchildren of a Mrs. Weymouth Schreiber (…) But if there is any of Sir Isaac's blood in Ontario, it may be that it is in the sons and grandchildren of Mrs. Weymouth Schreiber, whose husband moved to Springfield-on-the-Credit, and died there some years ago.

The Mrs. Weymouth Schreiber that "Sherbourne Street" referenced is not Weymouth's second wife Charlotte Schreiber, but his children's birth mother, Harriet DeLisle. After becoming aware of the inquiry in the newspaper during the same year, Schreiber's daughter Edith, known as Mrs. Quin in her response, replied to the issue from her home in England:

> In reply to Sherbourne Street's inquiry about Sir Isaac Brock's descendants, I can say that my mother, Mrs. Weymouth Schreiber, was a Miss. de Lisle, daughter of Captain de Lisle, and of Mary

> Carey of Guernsey (…) as our branch is the only one left in
> Canada I thought I should like to tell what I could, and may add
> that I lived in Guernsey as a child and knew and loved Sir Isaac
> Brock's beautiful little Island.

Unsatisfied with Edith's response, the unidentified writer demanded a clear answer regarding the relationship between Harriet DeLisle and Sir Isaac Brock:

> Mrs. Weymouth Schreiber was a Miss De Lisle, what relation was
> Mrs. Weymouth Schreiber to General Brock's mother? (…) there
> is another connection between the Schreibers and Brocks which
> has been allowed to obscure the issue which I raised.

Edith replied a final time. She stated that her mother, Harriet DeLisle, "was great grandniece of Elizabeth de Lisle, Sir Isaac Brock's mother."

Whatever scandal "Sherbourne Street" thought he had uncovered, Schreiber's only daughter put it to rest. Despite the foggy history of the land's ownership and speculations about the Brock-Schreiber family ties, the Schreiber family took possession of the beautiful wooded area on the Credit and started building.

2. Daily Life on the Credit

Ten years after moving to Canada, Weymouth Schreiber and his family left behind their busy lives in the growing city of Toronto and settled in Springfield-on-the-Credit. By this time, Schreiber's children were adults and had started families of their own. Schreiber's two sons, Weymouth George and Herbert Harrie, helped their father construct the three homes on the property, Mount Woodham, Iverholme and Lislehurst. According to Heritage Mississauga's "Erindale: The Crook of the Credit" tour brochure, Schreiber and his wife Charlotte occupied the Mount Woodham residence and eventually built a painter's studio inside the home for Charlotte. Charlotte named this house Mount Woodham after her childhood home in England. She is also credited for constructing the 105 steps from the house to the Credit River by herself.

Iverholme, a three-storey house built from wood and stone, belonged to Weymouth George and his family. Herbert Harrie, Weymouth Senior's second son, lived in Lislehurst, a two-and-half-storey house containing twelve windows and seven fireplaces. Herbert Harrie married Beatrice Mary Walker in 1882, and all five of their children were born in Lislehurst. Edith Schreiber continued to live at the family home in Toronto.

The three houses had no electricity, no running water and no telephone. Instead, a well with a pump, located in the yard, provided the family with drinking and bathing water. They also collected water in a cistern, an underground reservoir used to store rainwater, near the back door of Lislehurst. To maintain hygiene and cleanliness, the family bathed in a large tub beside one of the upstairs fireplaces. Without electricity, the family kept the house well-lit with coal oil lamps.

The family kept gardens on the property as well. At a cost of approximately $500 annually, the Schreibers grew their own vegetables, produced their own milk and cream, and stored ten barrels of apples, gathered from their apple orchard, for the winter months.

The Mount Woodham residence was also used as a school, where a governess taught Weymouth Schreiber's grandchildren.

The Schreiber family looked back on the time they spent on their 150-acre property with affection. In *Erindale at the Crook of the*

Credit, Adamson quotes Carol Schreiber, Herbert Harrie's daughter, about the family's experience living on the property:

> Carol thought that it was lovely to ride their horses 'through the trees and see the blue banks and flower flats' that surrounded the homes.
>
> Carol also remembers her father joking that he 'could walk across the river on the backs of the salmon' because the Credit River was bursting with fish."

While the Schreibers attained the property under what some believe were uncertain circumstances, the family lived comfortably on their wooded estate.

3. Charlotte Schreiber

At sixty-one years of age, Charlotte Schreiber still had the passion and drive of a young woman. In an article from *The Saturday Globe* dated Saturday March 2, 1895, a reporter recounts his journey to visit and interview the renowned artist at Mount Woodham.

> The first impression I had of Mrs. Schreiber was of a tall and active figure clad in a simple, neutral tinted gown, with a crown of rippling, snow-white hair shining in the strong sunlight and grey eyes lit up with summer lightning's of a soul. So fresh she looked, so sweet, so wholesome, and so kind that as I stood at length beneath her rooftree I gave not one regret to the discomfort which I had suffered upon the way.

Charlotte Mount Brock Morrell Schreiber was born in 1834 at Woodham Mortimer in Colchester in Essex, England to parents Reverend Robert Morell and Mary Mount Brock. The eldest of four children, Charlotte demonstrated a passion for art at a young age. At the time, most nineteenth-century fathers were reluctant to allow their daughters to receive an education, but Reverend Morrell supported Charlotte's artistic ambitions because he was an artist as well. At the age of sixteen, Charlotte's father arranged professional lessons for Charlotte at Mr. Carey's School of Art in London with painter John Rogers Herbert.

According to Joan Barrett and Gail Crawford's book *Extraordinary Lives: Inspiring Women of Peel,* Charlotte's art captured "figurative, sacred and historical subjects, along with studies of animals, children and portraits," a fairly popular art style at the time. Only five years later at twenty-one, Charlotte unveiled her artwork at an exhibit for the Royal Academy in London. This was the beginning of a life of artistic accomplishments.

In 1875, at the age of forty-one, Charlotte married her cousin Weymouth Schreiber and moved to Canada with him and his three children from a previous marriage.

In Canada, Charlotte achieved success. From 1876 to 1889, Charlotte served as an elected member of the Ontario Society of Art but was not allowed to vote at administrative meetings because of her gender. In 1877, Charlotte became the only woman on the teaching board at the Ontario School of Art and Design, now known as OCADU in Toronto, where for seven years she remained the only woman teaching and specializing in figure drawing and oil painting.

For her entire life, Charlotte's talent and passion laid in depicting detailed aspects of the human form. She spoke about her passion in an 1895 edition of *The Saturday Globe*: "The human hands, the fingernail, the foot, every portion of the living body, the part of a flower are divinely beautiful...it is a joy to paint them as they are in reality." Charlotte's interest in detailing the human form led her to create "The Croppy Boy (The Confession of an Irish Patriot)" in 1879, a painting that she used as her diploma picture for her election into the Royal Canadian Academy of Art. In the painting, now housed at the National Gallery of Canada in Ottawa, a young Irish rebel with cropped hair kneels at the feet of a priest and gives a confession. The priest, adorned in a blue hooded cloak, opens the garment to expose his officer uniform and true identity as a British spy.

This piece, along with a landscape painting titled "Springfield on the Credit"—which depicts the three Schreiber children bundled in winter outerwear and playing in the snow on a toboggan—are two of Charlotte's most famous works.

In 1880, Charlotte was elected as the first full female academician of the RCA. She was not allowed to attend meetings or, again, to vote for policy changes. Often, she would have her husband escort her to the RCA galas and address the audience on her behalf.

At home in Mount Woodham, Charlotte privately tutored students. She took particular interest in her student Ernest Thompson Seton, an author and artist. Barrett and Crawford's book reveals that Seton wrote *The Springfield Fox* and *Wild Animals I Have Known* while staying at Charlotte's residence and published the stories in 1898. The relationship between them developed into one beyond mentor-student, and the two became close friends, almost family. Seton often called Charlotte "Auntie Schreiber," and she would refer to him as "Dear Nephew."

Charlotte also introduced Herbert Harrie to his future wife Beatrice Mary, a fellow artist who often travelled from her home in Belleville to visit the Toronto Art Gallery, a gallery that Charlotte had helped to found.

Charlotte was also involved politically in her community. In 1898, she suggested Springfield-on-the-Credit change its name to Erindale after the residence where the family's neighbour and friend

Reverend James Magrath lived. A mailing mishap sparked the desire to rename the area. The residents of Springfield-on-the-Credit were annoyed that their mail was often sent to an American city with the same name. Magrath agreed, the town voted and Springfield-on-the Credit became known as Erindale.

Tragedy struck for the Schreiber clan in the late 1890s. In 1893, Ottillie, Weymouth George's wife, died leaving behind her husband and three young children. Only four years later, Herbert Harrie's wife Beatrice died after giving birth to the couple's fifth child. And just one year later, Charlotte experienced a loss of her own, when her husband passed away in 1898.

After the three consecutive deaths, the remaining Schreiber family scattered, abandoning their three extravagant homes and their lives in Erindale. Charlotte returned to England where she lived until her death in 1922 at the age of eighty-eight.

St. Peter's Anglican Church

Charlotte Schreiber and her husband, Weymouth, played a significant role in the rebuilding of St. Peter's Anglican Church, located on the corner of Dundas Street and Mississauga Road, in 1886, sixty years after its original construction.

Weymouth and fellow parishioners hauled stones from the Credit River up the hill to begin rebuilding the church. Charlotte sold paintings to raise money for the church. In particular, she sold her painting "Springfield on the Credit" that depicts the three Schreiber children clad in winter outerwear playing on a toboggan in the snow.

St. Peter's is home to Charlotte's oil on canvas painting of the original church and her rendition of the Ten Commandments and the Lord's Prayer in haunting Gothic script work.

Weymouth Schreiber is buried in the church's adjacent graveyard. The couple's contribution is integral to the history of St. Peter's Anglican Church.

Part II: Lislehurst After The Schreibers

According to local history, the Schreiber family left behind three enormous houses when they fled Erindale, and only Lislehurst has survived. Iverholme burned down in 1913, but the demise of Mount Woodham remains a mystery. Although the home appears in the historical records, an archaeological excavation that began in 2013 suggests it might never have been built.

4. Aftermath of Iverholme's Destruction

Dr. Walter McEwen rented Iverholme, the three-storey house constructed from stone and wood with ivy accents, as a summer estate after the Schreibers left the Erindale area. In 1913, while McEwen was away, a caretaker, identified as Stanley Plumb in Heritage Mississauga's "Schreiber Cottage Report" from 2006, was left to look after the property. Plumb was smoking his pipe on the porch when some of the hot ashes fell through the wooden boards and sparked a fire that engulfed the house in flames.

A black and white photograph from the Heritage Mississauga archives shows the destruction of the fire. All that remained of Iverholme was three storeys of scorched stone. The roof burned in the fire and the windows exploded.

Seventeen years later, on Tuesday January 28, 1930, an article for the *Toronto Daily Star* headlined "Beautiful Old Estate Might Become Subdivision" reported that the "beautiful Schreiber estate" had been sold. Valued at a purchase price of $40,000, realtor J. A. Willoughby negotiated the 1928 transaction on behalf of Reginald Watkins, a wealthy businessman and son to Thomas C. Watkins, who owned Right House, Hamilton's largest department store. At the time, Reginald Watkins was a retired merchant. Born in

Hamilton in 1877, Watkins attended school at the Upper Canada College. With one house destroyed by fire, Watkins purchased a property with two of three original Schreiber homes: Lislehurst and, supposedly, Mount Woodham.

Watkins' goal was to renovate Lislehurst in a Tudor style, a popular building trend in the 1920s that incorporated English architecture to give homes some medieval zest. Following the purchase of the land, Watkins journeyed to England and brought home European materials to begin crafting his new estate. After seventy trips to Europe, he modernized Lislehurst with "medieval carved beams in the ceilings [and] stone fireplaces" and imported wood panelling for the walls.

Formerly facing north towards the Credit River, Watkins reversed the orientation of Lislehurst during his renovations. He relocated the front entrance of the home so that Lislehurst would face south towards what is now the UTM campus. Today, the original entrance is the first floor powder room.

Unsatisfied with the size of Lislehurst, Watkins demolished Mount Woodham, the home where Charlotte Schreiber and her students had worked, and used the stone to add an extension on the west wing of Lislehurst.

The Lislehurst Heritage Structure Report, prepared on May 14, 1985 by Ian W. Scott, commissioner at the Mississauga Local Architectural Conservation Advisory Committee for Erindale College, describes the version of Lislehurst prior to Watkins' ownership as having tall windows and rich gingerbread trimmings.

Says the Heritage Report:

> The renovations of the 1920's involved removal of the gingerbread and an application, to both extensions and the original central

block, of an exposed timber and stucco finish. This complement to the stonework brought the visual effect up to the fashion of the 1920s […] an altogether appropriate style for the suburban estate of a wealthy city merchandiser.

But Watkins did not limit his renovation of the Schreiber estate to merely the interior and exterior of the house. To fully realize his medieval fantasy, Watkins altered the surrounding property as well. He constructed the long, curving gravel driveway, expansive lawns and even a bridge with a delicate pond that was featured decades later in many of the university's advertisements. An article in the December 22, 1963 edition of *The Globe and Mail,* "Bachelor Sold Fine Estate to University," reports that Watkins' property and landscape required seven maintenance staff to upkeep the estate.

Although little of Watkins' personal life has been documented, rumour at the time said this wealthy Hamilton-native enlarged and glorified Lislehurst in the hopes of winning the love of a woman, supposedly one of the five daughters of Sam McLaughlin, who founded the McLaughlin Motor Car Company, now known as General Motors of Canada, in 1907.

The same 1963 *The Globe and Mail* article reports that Watkins sold the property to the University of Toronto that July. The university agreed to allow Watkins to reside in Lislehurst for the rest of his life. He lived as a "recluse" until his death at eighty-six in December of 1963, leaving behind a niece, two nephews and "one of Canada's finest estates."

5. Where's Mount Woodham?

Donoghue offers me a ride back to campus after our tour of Lislehurst. He points out the 125 year old trees scattered along the property. I survey lawns blurring past Donoghue's car and think of Mount Woodham's demolition. Where were Mount Woodham and Iverholme in relation to Lislehurst? All my research provides me with vague descriptions—Mount Woodham and Lislehurst were "fairly close together" with Iverholme located just "across a ravine."

I arrange an interview with Dr. Michael Brand, historical archaeologist and sessional instructor in UTM's Anthropology Department, to discuss the potential locations of the other two houses. Since 2013, Brand's third and fourth year archaeological fieldwork classes have collected data on the property surrounding Lislehurst. Brand explains that while completing the surface collection, he and his team of students have found artefacts dating to the Schreibers' era.

"What we started doing is looking at the cultural landscape, the changes that the Schreibers made to the landscape to form it to their ideas of what the area should look like," he says. "There are a number of things like abandoned sections of road on the property. There's an old stone foundation near Lislehurst that we did a couple of seasons excavations at."

Brand has found evidence of the ruins of Iverholme's stone foundation but he has not figured out where Mount Woodham stood. Despite this, he is determined to continue his search.

"Watkins took Lislehurst and flipped the house around," Brand explains. "He tore down Mount Woodham, so the story goes, and apparently used the materials to enlarge Lislehurst, but everything I found so far suggests that Woodham was a brick house, not a stone house, so it doesn't quite match with him using the materials to do that."

Brand explains that on the site of the remaining Iverholme foundation, there is significantly less stone available than what was pictured after the accident in the 1913 photographs. Based on the evidence of human activity in the area near the house, such as empty beer cans and garbage cans charcoaled from fire, Brand proposes two possibilities to explain the missing stone. The stone was either stolen by members of the community, homeless individuals or the general public, or the "stone" Reginald Watkins used to enlarge Lislehurst actually came from the ruins of Iverholme.

But could members of the community really steal an entire stone foundation of a house?

Matthew Wilkinson, the historian at Heritage Mississauga and a colleague of Brand's, explains that even when a house is torn down, it is extremely difficult to erase the foundation it has left on the land. Wilkinson reveals that he often jokes with Brand about how he's wasting his time searching for a "ghost house"—a house that may have never really existed.

Wilkinson proposes his own theory about the missing house. He believes that there may have only been two houses, Lislehurst and one other. The lack of physical evidence leads Wilkinson to believe that the second house may have undergone a name change, from Mount Woodham to Iverholme, resulting in a mistake in the historical record.

Interestingly, this is not the first instance of misinformation about Lislehurst. The notion that the property was originally owned by General Brock and then handed to the Schreibers is an ahistorical "fact" that took root because people repeated it so often. (The fact is that Sir Isaac Brock died without ever having possessed the land.) Perhaps a similar mistake occurred in recording this history.

Four years of archaeological digging has led to nothing but dead ends. While Brand has found no physical evidence of a third house on the grounds, he has found remnants of an incinerator used to burn garbage, fragmented pieces of ceramic dolls, headless toy soldiers and a lid from a jar with a marking from Harrison China House, a distributor in Toronto.

What then are the consequences of incorrectly documented history? What happens to a story, to a family, to a house, when the truth of its history becomes mangled, fragmented and lost in the passage of time? What is a place if it doesn't have a history?

I have lived in Erindale for my entire life. Why have I never heard of Lislehurst or the Schreiber family? Brand doesn't think students' unawareness of Lislehurst correlates with the value the school places on this historic site. "It's tucked in behind buildings and modern housing," Brand explains. "I don't think it's a disconnect with heritage that's keeping people out of here. People are so busy with what they're doing that they don't even know it exists."

6. Lislehurst's Legacy

In September 1967, Erindale College opened its doors to 155 students, and Lislehurst became the college's designated private residence for J. Tuzo Wilson, the college's first principal. As each new principal was elected, from Wilson to Ulrich Krull, Lislehurst became home to many different residents.

An email located in the UTM archives shows Ian Orchard's investigation into the meaning of the name "Lislehurst." The response, dated from 2007, came from a woman named Lisa Boyle. She provides Orchard with some research on the name from a site called *Ontario Architecture*. The name can be broken into two parts: Lisle: originating from a family name, perhaps Louisa DeLisle, and Hurst: "a residence that borders the wood." Based on the history of the property's ownership and observations of the wooded area that sur-rounds the residence, the combination is fitting.

From 2002 to 2010, Orchard served as the Vice-President University of Toronto and Principal of University of Toronto Mississauga. During his time at UTM, Orchard and his wife Angela resided in Lislehurst and worked towards treating the remarkable house as a community possession and not solely as their private living quarters. Orchard agreed to a telephone interview to discuss his time in the home and the impact of living in a heritage building.

Prior to Orchard and his wife's arrival in 2002, the university had to replace Lislehurst's cedar shingle roof after water leaked into the upstairs washroom. The new roof matched the damaged one—a requirement made clear in the 1985 City of Mississauga heritage designation that forbids modifications to the exterior of Lislehurst unless for maintenance purposes. The heritage designation allows owners to modify the interior, but Orchard and Donoghue, inter-ested in preserving the character of the home, hired craftsmen to decorate the inside of the house according to 1880s fashions. They lined the staircase and the back corridor with a material made to look like marble, which strengthened the historic feel of the home.

Although today most students are unaware of Lislehurst, during Orchard's tenure as principal, he was keen on opening the house to the community of UTM: the faculty, staff and students. Orchard held receptions in Lislehurst for various student groups, such as in-ternational students, athletes and residence dons. For each event, Orchard gave a five- to ten-minute account of the history of the house to remind the community that although UTM is a relatively young campus, celebrating its fiftieth anniversary in 2017, the build-ing's history dates back to 1885.

"I'll tell you a funny story, we had a family dinner there for Thanksgiving one weekend, and we were cooking our turkey and actually eating our turkey, and we look up and there's a woman with her face against the window, peering at us," Orchard says, and laughs. "And then the front door opens and a man walks in, and they assumed this was an open museum historic home and they came for a tour. That was sort of amusing. We had a lot of what we would call 'tourists.' People would drive by and stop and take pictures."

For Orchard and his wife Angela, living in such a historic house was different than what they were used to. Coming from relatively simple backgrounds, Orchard and his wife made sure to take advantage of every room in the mansion.

"It was relatively temporary but we were in a privileged position to experience such a magnificent home that was built so long ago," Orchard says. He believes timing and circumstance play a large role in why students aren't aware of Lislehurst.

"The next principal may go back to the ideology that the house belongs to the community," Orchard says. "It's hard for a small family to live in a house that's so big without assuming the house really belongs to the community."

Lislehurst has hosted many events for members of the external community as well. Orchard mentions that Premier Dalton McGuinty held his first cabinet meeting with his MPs at the house.

Lislehurst embodies the essence of Victorian privilege. A back staircase leads to the attic, the sleeping area of the butler and maid. In the basement, the original wires still hang down with labels like "butler's room" that the Schreiber family used to ring the servants.

"Living in the house made us reflect on how privileged some people have been and are," Orchard explains. "It's fascinating that an era like that existed. So I think when you live in a house you see a reflection of history and class structure and that's sort of interesting to get that perspective."

Conclusion: Discovering Fact

The archives at UTM collect all manner of documents related to the campus history, but not all the documents have attributions. Whoever tore a 1963 letter to the editor about Lislehurst from a newspaper did not preserve the name of that newspaper.

The letter is written by Enid Schreiber, one of Herbert Harrie's daughters. She wrote to correct errors in a previously published article about the grounds of Erindale College.

Schreiber, signing as Mrs. C. Swanson, from her home in Vancouver, British Columbia, wrote:

> Lislehurst, where I was born seventy-six years ago, you describe as being built thirty years ago. Actually, Mr. Watkins only made a few improvements with the stone from my uncle's house which was burned down some years before. You say the estate was bush-land when Mr. Watkins bought it, but in our time it was a lovely country place like an English home. There were tennis courts and a lovely view looking north over the Mullett Creek and the Credit River.

This letter is an integral piece in the history of Lislehurst. Enid Schreiber, granddaughter of Weymouth Schreiber and an original resident of the home, reveals in her reply that Watkins built the extension to Lislehurst with the "stone from [her] uncle's house which was burned down some years before." Her uncle, Weymouth George, lived in Iverholme, the house that was destroyed in the fire in 1913.

The newspapers from Watkins' 1930 purchase report that he used the stone from Mount Woodham. Enid Schreiber's response directly contradicts the widely known tale of Watkins' demolition of Mount Woodham to enlarge Lislehurst and instead states that the material came from Iverholme. Does this confirm the theory that there were only two houses?

I think about the similarities between Enid Schreiber and myself as I dig through my scribbled research notes, photographs of news articles from archives and electronic documents from Heritage Mississauga in an attempt to put the pieces together of the puzzle that is the history of Lislehurst.

Through our writing we both challenge accepted facts and work towards setting the record straight. Enid Schreiber, a seventy-six-year-old original resident of the home, wrote into the local newspaper to correct an article dated Thursday July 18, 1963. I, a twenty-year-old student attending the university that was built upon the land her family called home, conduct research and interviews with professors of archaeology, local historians and modern day residents of the homes to understand what it was like to live in Lislehurst and to discover if there were truly three houses at all.

Rewriting history is difficult, but we make the effort to tell the true story.

So what does happen to a story, to a family, to a house, when the truth of its history becomes lost in the passage of time? It's simple. People take the most easily accessible facts as concrete truth.

From the nineteenth-century news reports to the 1905 anonymous accusatory inquiry to the reoccurring belief that Watkins demolished Mount Woodham for a Lislehurst expansion, people believe myth rather than attempt to seek out the facts. It is important to preserve historic records because false records will lead to false understandings.

Enid Schreiber ends her letter to the editor with one simple statement: "The history of this property is Canadian history."

I agree. The history of this property is Canadian history, but it's my campus's history too. I want to tell as true a story as the facts will allow.

Select Chronology

1861   Lousia DeLisle forecloses on Edward Shortiss' mortgage on the property.

1869   Louisa DeLisle gives the property as a gift in trust to the children of Weymouth Schreiber and his first wife Harriet DeLisle.

1875   Weymouth and his second wife, established English artist Charlotte Mount Brock Morrell (age 41), along with his three children from his first marriage, immigrate to Canada. They built a large estate in Toronto and summer houses in Erindale.

1885   The Schriebers construct three houses: Mount Woodham, Iverholm, Lislehurst.

1898   Charlotte suggests Springfield-on-the-Credit change its name to Erindale because post office confuses Springfield-on-the-Credit with other towns named Springfield.

1898   Weymouth Schreiber dies and Charlotte returns to England.

1913   Iverholme "accidentally" burns down.

1928   Reginald Watkins, wealthy businessman from Hamilton, purchases property. Watkins tore down Mount Woodham and used the stone to enlarge Lislehurst. He added a west wing and reversed the orientation of the house (originally the front of the house faced the Credit River).

1963   University of Toronto purchases the property a year after Watkins dies and Lislehurst becomes the private residence of the college's principal.

2013   Dr. Michael Brand begins archaeological field work on the property to discover evidence of Mount Woodham and Iverholme's location – and reaches many dead ends. Evidence suggests the possibility of only two original houses on the property, Lislehurst and Iverholme/Mount Woodham.

Sources

(N.A) (1905). The Brock Family (Sherbourne Street Inquiry). Located in the *UTM Library Archives Lislehurst Newspaper File.*

(N.A) (1930, 28 January). Beautiful Old Estate Might Become Subdivision. *Toronto Daily Star.* Located in the *UTM Library Archives Lislehurst Newspaper File.*

(N.A) (1963, 22 December). Bachelor Sold Fine Estate to University. *The Globe and Mail.* Located in the *UTM Library Archives Lislehurst Newspaper File.*

(N.A) (n.d). General Brock's Relatives Sell 40-Acre Farm. Located in the *UTM Library Archives Lislehurst Newspaper File.*

(N.A) (n.d). Pioneer Family Capitalists: Schreiber Family, Relatives of Sir Isaac Brock leaving Homestead, REG. WATKINS BUYER. Located in the *UTM Library Archives Lislehurst Newspaper File.*

(N.A). (1895). *The Saturday Globe.* Located in the *UTM Principal Lislehurst Binder.*

(N.A). (n.d). The Schreibers of Local History. Located in the *UTM Library Archives Lislehurst Newspaper File.*

Adamson, J. (1978). *Erindale at the Crook of the Credit.* Canada: The Boston Mills Press.

Bach, V. and Ungar M. P. (2005). Morrell, Charlotte Mount Brock (Schreiber). *Dictionary of Canadian Biography,* vol. 15. University of Toronto/Universite Laval. Retrieved from http://www.biographi.ca/en/bio/8305?revision_id=6078

Barrett, J. and Crawford, G. (2012). *Extraordinary Lives: Inspiring Women of Peel.* Orillia: Rose Printing.

Brand, M. Historical Archeologist and Sessional Instructor in University of Toronto Mississauga's Anthropology Department. (2017, 14 Feburary) About location of Mount Woodham. [In-person interview].

Clarkson, G. C. (1963, October). The History of the Grounds Comprising the New West Campus of the University of Toronto at Erindale. *UTM Library Archives.* Retrieved from http://www.utm.utoronto.ca/library/facilities/pdfs/historygrounds.pdf

Concordia University. (n.d). Schreiber, Charlotte. *Canadian Women Artists History Initiative.* Retrieved from http://cwahi.concordia.ca/sources/artists/displayArtist.php?ID_artist=40

Crucefix, L. (n.d). History of Campus. *Office of the Vice-President and Principal.* Retrieved from https://www.utm.utoronto.ca/vp-principal/history-campus

Donoghue, P. Chief Administrative Officer University of Toronto Mississauga. (2017, 14 February). Tour of Lislehurst.

Friend, M. (1983). Erindale's Own Artist: Charlotte Schreiber (1834-1922). *UTM Library Archives.* Retrieved from https://tspace.library.utoronto.ca/bitstream/1807/44103/1/charlotteschreiber.pdf

Heritage Mississauga. (2006). Schreiber's Cottage Report: Preservation of the Subject Property as a component of the University of Toronto at Mississauga prepared for Professor Henry Halls. *Heritage Mississauga Archives.*

Heritage Mississauga. (2007). Charlotte Mount Brock Schreiber. *Heritage News: The Newsletter of Heritage Mississauga,* vol.20, issue 1. Retrieved from http://www.heritagemississauga.com/assets/Winter%202007.pdf

Heritage Mississauga. (2010). A Heritage Tour Erindale "The Crook of the Credit". *Erindale Heritage Tour Brochure.* Retrieved from http://www.heritagemississauga.com/assets/Erindale%20Heritage%20Tour%20Brochure%20-%20Final%20-%202011.pdf

Heritage Mississauga. (n.d). Erindale. *Heritage Mississauga.* Retrieved from http://www.heritagemississauga.com/page/Erindale

Heritage Mississauga. (n.d). Schreiber, Charlotte. *Heritage Mississauga.* Retrieved from http://www.heritagemississauga.com/page/Charlotte-Schreiber

Historic Places. (n.d). Lislehurst. *Canada's Historic Places.* Retrieved from http://www.historicplaces.ca/en/rep-reg/place-lieu.aspx?id=14962

Iverholme after 1913 Fire [photograph]. Mississauga, ON: Heritage Mississauga.

Library and Archives Canada. (n.d). Charlotte Mount Brock Schreiber. *Celebrating Women's Achievements.* Retrieved from https://www.collectionscanada.gc.ca/women/030001-1170-e.html

National Gallery of Canada. (n.d). Charlotte Schreiber 1834 – 1922. *Collections*. Retrieved from https://www.gallery.ca/en/see/collections/artist.php?iartistid=4938

Orchard, I. Vice-President Academic and Provost of the University of Waterloo. (2017, 17 Feburary). About time spent living in Lislehurst. [Telephone interview].

Parkwood Estate. (n.d). RSM Story. *The R.S McLaughlin Estate National Historic Site*. Retrieved from http://www.parkwoodestate.com/learn/rsm-story/

Ryan, C. A. M. (2012). Charlotte Schreiber (1834-1922). *Blackwood Gallery University of Toronto Mississauga*. Retrieved from http://www.blackwoodgallery.ca/Web%20Images/Permanent%20Collection/PDF/Charlotte%20Schreiber.pdf

Schreiber, Charlotte [photograph]. Mississauga, ON: Heritage Mississauga.

Schreiber, Enid. (1963). Letters to the Editor's Desk: Reader Brings History of New University Grounds up to date. Located in the *UTM Library Archives Lislehurst Newspaper File*.

Scott, I. W. (1985, 14 May). Heritage Structure Report prepared for Erindale College. *Architectural Conservation Advisory Committee*. Located in the *UTM Principal Lislehurst Binder*.

Stasierowski, M. (1980). Lislehurst: House of Many Phases, Part Two. *Medium II*, vol.7, no.12. Retrieved from https://archive.org/details/mediumii07n12erin

Wilkinson, M. (2010). Inquiry Response Letter. *Heritage Mississauga Archives.*

Wilkinson, M. (n.d). Lislehurst Timeline: Clarifying a Local Legend. *Heritage Mississauga Archives.*

ACKNOWLEDGEMENTS

We are indebted to the vibrant history available to us in Ontario and to the people who keep it alive, in particular Heritage Mississauga and its historian Matthew Wilkinson; the archives of the University of Toronto and City of Mississauga; and the many people who the writers of these stories interviewed. Thank you to Laurie Kallis for editorial advice, cover design, layout, moral support and everything else she does for Life Rattle. Thank you also to Dr. Margaret Proctor and Dr. Tracy Moniz, who taught History and Writing and produced peer model texts that we used as a model for this volume of stories. Thank you, too, to Dr. Guy Allen for his leadership and support. An earlier version of the essay in the introduction was first published online by Troy Media.